WHAT YOUR COLLEAGUES AR

How magical it was to watch my seventh graders go from "I don't like poetry" and "I can't write poetry" to, two days later, confidently stating, "I'm a poet!" Using the poems and structures, students felt empowered and successful! The poems made sense and inspired them to write their own.

—**Marie Cleary**
Seventh-Grade Teacher, ATLAS Academy, Waco, TX

I had a *blast* with these lessons. We partnered up; each child was able to talk or read what they wrote for two minutes each. We then read the poem of the lesson and discussed how students could relate. Then the students began writing their own poems. I totally loved the outcomes. My students rocked the lessons!

—**Stacy Sauerwein**
Fourth-Grade Teacher, Dripping Springs Elementary School, Dripping Springs, TX

The poetry exercises are accessible, enriching, and easy to work with for students and teachers. The activities are constructed in a way that helps students understand the structure, theme, and tone of the model poem while providing a substantive framework to begin their own work. If teachers are looking for ways to introduce poetry to students that satisfies both how poems are made and how to craft their own, there is no better text today.

—**Dameion Wagner**
11th-Grade Teacher, Columbus, OH

Using poetry as a vehicle to critically examine and connect experiences is such a phenomenal way of getting students to pay attention to their insights as active readers. These lessons motivate students to not only evaluate the text itself, but also to evaluate their thinking meta-cognitively. Highly engaging and student centered, the lessons integrate cultural responsiveness authentically.

—**Tracye Thomas**
Instructional Coach, Channelview ISD, Channelview, TX

Text Structure
every teache.
and a love of poetry. Gretchen Be......
Prooyen have given teachers an entire book of high-density, academic poems from which to choose with every level of student. These two master teachers help us to understand how to take kids through the "back door" of reading and analyzing poetry, and before you know it, your students will become experts in discussing and writing about structure, literary devices, theme, tone, rhyme scheme and diction. I am excited about using this book with AP students, on-level students, and students who may be intimidated by poetry. The process is simple, and the results are amazing!

—**Dottie Hall**
High School Teacher/Principal, Northside ISD, San Antonio, TX

When I was led through this strategy, at first I wasn't optimistic and knew without a doubt I would not be raising my hand to share. I blew myself away with what I accomplished in a mere ten minutes. To say the step-by-step guidelines made it easy is an understatement. I can hardly wait to show teachers how easily they will be able to build poetry writing confidence in their students.

—**Lorraine Young**
Secondary ESL Coordinator, Cypress-Fairbanks ISD, Houston, TX

Text Structures From Poetry does for students what many curricula and teachers fail to do: make poetry engaging and approachable without missing the beautiful, miraculous nature of a poem. Oh yeah, and it's fun.

—**John Spiegel**
Seventh-Grade Teacher, Springfield, OH

GRADES 4-12

Text Structures From Poetry

GRADES 4–12

Text Structures From Poetry

Lessons to Help Students Read, Analyze, and Create Poems They Will Remember

Includes 50 Lessons and Mentor Texts

Gretchen Bernabei
Laura Van Prooyen

CORWIN Literacy

For information:

Corwin
A SAGE Company
2455 Teller Road
Thousand Oaks, California 91320
(800) 233–9936
www.corwin.com

SAGE Publications Ltd.
1 Oliver's Yard
55 City Road
London EC1Y 1SP
United Kingdom

SAGE Publications India Pvt. Ltd.
B 1/I 1 Mohan Cooperative Industrial Area
Mathura Road, New Delhi 110 044
India

SAGE Publications Asia-Pacific Pte. Ltd.
18 Cross Street #10–10/11/12
China Square Central
Singapore 048423

Director and Publisher,
    Corwin Classroom: Lisa Luedeke
Editorial Development Manager: Julie Nemer
Senior Editorial Assistant: Sharon Wu
Production Editor: Melanie Birdsall
Typesetter: Integra
Proofreader: Lawrence W. Baker
Cover and Interior Designer: Gail Buschman
Marketing Manager: Deena Meyer

Library of Congress Cataloging-in-Publication Data

Names: Bernabei, Gretchen S., author. | Van Prooyen, Laura, author.
Title: Text structures from poetry, grades 4-12 : lessons to help students read, analyze, and create poems they will remember / Gretchen Bernabei, Laura Van Prooyen.
Description: Thousand Oaks, California : Corwin Press, Inc. [2020] | Identifiers: LCCN 2019040860 | ISBN 9781544384856 (paperback)
Subjects: LCSH: Poetry—Study and teaching (Elementary)—Activity programs. | Poetry—Study and teaching (Secondary)—Activity programs.
Classification: LCC PN1101 .B46 2020 | DDC 372.64/044—dc23 LC record available at https://lccn.loc.gov/2019040860

Printed in the United States of America

This book is printed on acid-free paper.

22 23 24 10 9 8 7 6 5 4 3 2

Contents

CLASSIC POEMS　　101

APPENDICES 214

Visit the companion website at
resources.corwin.com/textstructures-poetry
for a full glossary, downloadable text structures,
and additional resources.

Acknowledgments

We owe many thanks to the incomparable Lisa Luedeke and our Corwin team: Julie Nemer, Sharon Wu, Melanie Birdsall, and Gail Buschman. And our home team, Judi Reimer, Fran Awbry, Jayne Hover, Marian Jones, Dottie Hall, Onnie Aguirre, Ida Valdez, Lorraine Young, Honor Moorman, Catherine McGough, Amy Doege, and Kevin Gillaspie. To Kim Grauer and Morgan Kern and their guidance with the classics.

We are especially indebted to the following teachers who tried out lessons in their classrooms and tracked down permission slips, and whose students are published in this volume: Stacy Sauerwein, Leslie Lindsay, Kelly Redies, Barbara Ryan, Zachary Wilson, Lynn Jarzombek, Kerri Saulmon, Jennifer Porter, Eva Nelson, Stephanie Cash, Tracie Knodel, Matthew Guess, Dalton Foster, Shaniea Pennygraph-Compaore, Kat Sauter, Melissa Quintanilla-Vasquez, Angela Applegate, Eric Cruz, Nathan Dupont, Regenna Mendoza, John Spiegel, and Dana Williams.

Thank you to the playful and spirited adults who shared their poems too: Carol Mendenhall, Sandy Boydston, Sue King, Patricia Sue Gray, and Lorrie Payne.

From Gretchen: I'm also grateful for the following influences: Dina Toland, Kathy Bieser, Tiffany Jenkins, Gina Graham, Laura Sisson, Becky Ebner Hoag, Nicole Morales, Melissa Skinner, Nanette Raska, Carol Booth Olson, Alana Morris, Susan Diaz, Jeannie Istre, Claudia Sharp, Greg Reeves, Craigg Woodman, Michele St. John, Kreisti Bunch, Jennifer Payne, Lynda Morgart, Stephanie Vaughn, Maureen Ucles, Jim Burke, Tim Martindell, Marie Cleary, Heather Dollins, the McWhorter family, and of course, Matilde and Julian, Bert and Dixie. And also for Laura: When do we get started on the lame version?

From Laura: I wish to thank Tim, Sadie, Jessie, and Ivy. (Every. Single. Day.) Thanks to my poetry friends and colleagues who eagerly contributed their work to this book, and to the people and places who gave me the chance to teach most recently: Sheila Black, Alexandra Van De Kamp, and Florinda Brown from Gemini Ink; Tookie Spoor and Frank Alfaro for entrusting me with the Martha Spoor Young Writers Workshop; Keith Tuma from Miami University MFA Program for Creative Writing; Jeffrey Flores from our Henry Ford Academy: Alameda School of Art + Design days; Amy Stengel for the visiting writer gig; Captain Richard Schobitz, Dr. Gerard Grace, and Roy Gissendanner, who saw the difference poetry and writing made with soldiers at Brook Army Medical Center; and Jen Osborne for our shared mission. And of course, Gretchen Bernabei, who—thanks to serendipity and the forces of the universe—poured me a cup of coffee, took me on a tour of a school, and within thirty minutes asked me to co-author this book. I am so grateful for our friendship, questionable humor, and for the many containers of plantain chips that fueled us as we put together this book.

PUBLISHER'S ACKNOWLEDGMENTS

Corwin gratefully acknowledges the contributions of the following reviewers:

Krista Geffre
Secondary Humanities Teacher and Graduate Consultant
Frontier Charter Academy
Hillsboro, OR

Carmen Gordillo
Middle School Teacher and Adjunct Professor
Rutgers University
Union City, NJ

Viviana Tamas
Reading Teacher and Literacy Coach
White Plains, NY

Introduction

I'll admit it. I (Gretchen) have never done a good job teaching poetry. I've read some poems I loved and let students write poetry (that I occasionally loved), but I've never been confident about showing them how to deeply analyze a poem or how to write a poem to be proud of.

Apparently, I haven't been alone. If you're a parent, what poems have your children brought home from school? Year after year, you might see a haiku, a cinquain, a diamante, an acrostic poem, maybe a "where I'm from" poem, and then we're out of time—oh well, we've covered poetry.

Lately, I've been thinking about my poetry insecurity, touching my finger onto the sore spot and pushing, and ruminating on several points. *Maybe I've avoided teaching poetry because it's so broad, and my expertise with it is so spotty. Maybe I don't like to parade my insecurities before students, so I spend more class time minutes teaching them how to do things I really do well, and poetry gets short shrift.*

And then the arguments (with myself) begin in earnest.

Truthfully, I do love some poems. In fact, my own personal relationships with poems have been individual and intense. I embraced "My Last Duchess" the moment that my sister Sue whirled around in the front seat of the car in the Kubasaki High School parking lot and soothed my broken teenage heart by reading it to me, showing me how cruel the world can be to gentle people. And I've continued to see the powers of a well-placed poem when my own words aren't powerful enough for a situation. For instance, when another teacher is weary from the daily slings and arrows, there's no talisman like Naomi Nye's "Kindness." Poetry can serve so many purposes: it can incite us to action; poetry can heal.

But these personal experiences with the health benefits of poetry have not translated into competence in teaching the world of poetry to students. Looking around to see how others teach poetry, I've seen some dismal sights: worksheets, dissections, groan-filled packets of figurative language overkill. I've watched eye-rolling adolescents holding their breath as enraptured adults perform some verse or other, unaware that their invitation to the pleasure will never convince any but the two front-row teacher pleasers, about whom later the teachers will purr, " ... and they loved it." These approaches have made me recoil from poetry. Billy Collins clarified it for me in his poem "Introduction to Poetry," describing what happens to poems at the hands of teachers: we tie them to chairs and torture them until they're dead.

I don't want to damage poems or children; I want to *first do no harm.* And so my own Hippocratic teaching oath leads me to avoid fake-teaching poetry. I'd rather teach no poetry than do damage.

So that's the conundrum. As a result, I've turned my attention throughout the years to finding more effective ways to light a prose-writing fire in students, a quest that has kept me occupied for more than 30 years.

And then my poetry world shifted on its axis: I crossed paths with the poet Laura Van Prooyen. She had come to my school, thanks to a grant through Gemini Ink, our gem of a local writers' organization, for a six-week series of poetry writing with sixth graders. When she arrived, I gave her a tour and a cup of coffee, and we shared some of our beliefs and processes. Within the hour, she was explaining to me how she likes to have students look at the way a poem is built in order to emulate that structure in their own poetry. I knew then I'd met a kindred teaching spirit; I told her about my similar focus on structures in other genres and how we teach students to use and eventually choose their own structures when writing any discourse.

Laura surprised me. She teaches children and adults, even her MFA poetry graduate students, to, as she says, "pop the hood on a poem and take a look at the engine." *How does it work? How does one part relate to the other parts? What makes this engine run?*

They look at the mechanics, like rhyme scheme and formation, but most of all, they look at the movement of the parts. The *structure* of the text.

That morning, I joined a group of sixth graders and a couple of their parents as Laura had everyone choose a jellybean, and we were off on a poetry adventure as the flavor of the jellybean led us to memories and a new relationship with Joanne Diaz's "My Mother's Tortilla." I heard myself thinking *I can do this* as I wrote my own poem.

And then we created this book together. I learned to use my well-known tools to read and write poetry, and to learn about the magic of poetry from the poems themselves.

Before we get into the lessons, though, I have to tell you one fascinating thing that I learned from Laura: Don't get her started on a poem's "hidden meaning." Okay, too late. Laura wishes she could say the following to every teacher:

> *Please stop telling students to find the poem's hidden meaning.*
>
> *Poets don't write to be confusing.*
>
> *Poets don't write to frustrate someone with a hidden meaning.*
>
> *Good poems might have multiple meanings, or maybe you get more meaning when you read it more.*
>
> *Unanswerable questions are not the same as a hidden meaning.*
>
> *Poets write so that someone else can understand something, in hopes of a human connection.*
>
> *Most poets strive for clarity of thought, in one way or another.*

Just ask a poet about her "hidden meaning," and you may be in for a rant.

HOW TO USE THIS BOOK

Look through the contents and shop for a poem that looks good to you, or browse through the lessons, looking at their structures to help you decide which ones to choose.

The lessons we included show you how to have students read and write a poem. Because we wanted to streamline the lessons for simplicity, we did not go into the lives of the poets, their contributions, or their thoughts about their work. However, in the appendices you will find some fascinating and juicy messages from the contemporary poets in "Meet the Contemporary Authors."

LESSON SEQUENCE

Every lesson has a page of Teaching Notes that we use to lead students through the following process.

1. **Freewrite about the topic for two or three minutes.** The idea here is nobody starts with a blank page, and this prevents the "I don't have anything to write about" problem that could come up later. Some teachers have told us that they ask students to share with a partner at this stage; if there's an odd number of students, the teacher takes a partner and shares too. Then put this freewriting aside. The students won't be obligated to use this later, but they might. The purpose is to get their synapses firing.

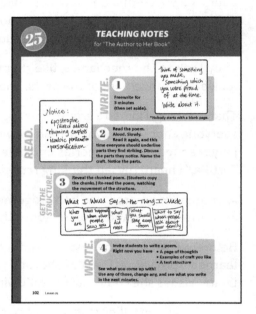

2. **Now it's time to distribute copies of the poem and look at the poem.** Read the title together with the students. Think together about what the title tells you.

3. **Read the poem aloud.** Read it slowly, just to hear what it does, what it says.

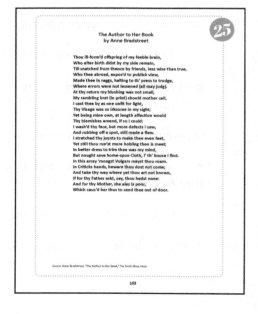

4. **Re-read the poem aloud again, and this time, ask the students to write on their copies of the poem as you read, highlighting any parts that strike them, or any craft they notice.** After reading, compare notes about what they marked. Tell them names of what they notice where possible. (Our notes are on the Teaching Notes page, with explanations of terms provided in the glossary.)

5. **Now it's time to show them the structure.** On a document camera or projector, show them the poem all chunked up. Ask them to copy the chunking and the text structure onto their copy of the poem.

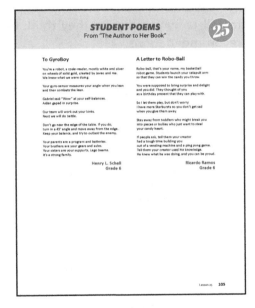

6. **Re-read the poem one more time.** Ask them to watch the movement of the text structure as you go through the poem.

7. **Give the students about 10 minutes to write their own poem.** They may choose to use **any** parts of their freewriting, or any of this poet's craft, or the text structure. (They may also choose to change any of these.)

While this sequence provides a solid experience weaving writing and reading together, there are plenty of variations that could also prove useful:

For instance, do steps 1, 3, 4, then 2:

- Freewrite
- Look at the text structure
- Create a poem
- Then share the published poem
- Identify some craft and try that same craft on the writing

Or … use the structure to write some prose, like a letter, an essay, or a speech.

Or … use the structure to write a response poem.

Or … read the poem and write a one-sentence summary of each box in the structure, as a way to summarize, or kernelize, the poem.

Or … have students take an unmarked poem and do all of the chunking to discover the structure on their own.

TIMING THE LESSON

With students (Grades 4–12) we've worked with, the whole lesson takes 40–55 minutes.

Revisions can take one or more sessions or can go on indefinitely.

We like to have student draft lots of poems and polish up their choices for publication in any number of ways (on the wall, in student anthologies, online).

What do you do with student poetry after it's written?

Students should have plenty of opportunity to play with what they've written, and we've shared some of our favorite ideas in the appendices.

How did we pick THESE poems?

For the contemporary section, we wanted to include a wide representation of a broad range of voices who are keen observers of the world. And we think they emulate the qualities of great poetry, qualities that we think would be great models for young writers.

For the poems from earlier times, we asked some of our favorite English teachers to tell us which poems they think every student should read. We really liked their recommendations.

After you've used these lessons, you'll discover you don't need the book any more. You can use the same (or your own personalized) process to teach any poem you love.

How do we know our text structures are what the poets were thinking?

We don't. The poem chunks seemed clear to us, but these are arbitrary divisions. You might kernelize the poem differently. On a different day, so might we. But our aim is to provide students with a workable, manageable structure that we see clearly in the poems, in hopes that they will not only find these structures useful for writing but also to help train their eyes to spot structures as they read on their own, to become natural chunkers. To reduce their fear of the word "analysis" by learning how to do it first. To teach them to pop the hood on the poem to see how it works, and to trust their eyes when they look under that hood.

We don't want to tie up a poem onto a chair; we'd rather teach children to look at a poem and read it with a light touch. If we feel confident teaching children to read and write poems like that, then we may not avoid teaching poetry. As a result, our students will read and produce poetry that they can be proud of. I wish I'd had this book years ago, and we hope you enjoy using it now.

Lessons

Contemporary Poems

WRITE.

1 Freewrite for 3 minutes (then set aside).

> Think of a place you like to go because it makes you feel good when you go there.
> Write for a few minutes about that place and all the things you might see and experience there.

Nobody starts with a blank page.

READ.

Notice:
- time changes
- how conjunctions move the poem (and now, but)
- those italics!

2 Read the poem. Aloud. Slowly.
Read it again, and this time everyone should underline parts they find striking. Discuss the parts they notice. Name the craft. Notice the parts.

GET THE STRUCTURE.

3 Reveal the chunked poem. (Students copy the chunks.) Re-read the poem, watching the movement of the structure.

Acting On Impulse

| things I see that make me feel/think/react | What I wish I could say | but how the world expects us to react | Instead, I decide to do/say ___. | the reaction I get |

WRITE.

4 Invite students to write a poem.
Right now you have
- A page of thoughts
- Examples of craft you like
- A text structure

See what you come up with!
Use any of those, change any, and see what you write in the next minutes.

Love Waltz With Fireworks
by Kelli Russell Agodon

Seventeen minutes ago, I was in love
    with the cashier and a cinnamon pull-apart,
    seven minutes before that, it was a gray-

haired man in argyle socks, a woman
    dancing outside the bakery holding
    a cigarette and broken umbrella. The rain,

I've fallen in love with it many times,
    the fog, the frost—how it covers the clovers
    —and by clovers I mean lovers.

And now I'm thinking how much I want to rush up
    to the stranger in the plaid wool hat
    and tell him how much I love his eyes,

all those fireworks, every seventeen minutes, exploding
    in my head—you the baker, you the novelist,
    you the reader, you the homeless man on the corner

with the strong hands—I've thought about you. But
    in this world we've been taught to keep
    our emotions tight, a rubberband ball we worry

if one band loosens, the others will begin shooting off
    in so many directions. So we quiet.
    I quiet. I eat my cinnamon bread

in the bakery watching the old man still sitting
    at his table, moving his napkin as he drinks
    his small cup of coffee, and I never say,

I think you're beautiful, except in my head,
    except I decide I can't
    live this way, and walk over to him and

place my hand on his shoulder, lean in close
    and whisper, *I love your argyle socks*,
    and he grabs my hand,

the way a memory holds tight in the smallest
    corner. He smiles and says,
    I always hope someone will notice.

Source: "Love Waltz With Fireworks" previously published in *ONE: Jacar Press.* Reprinted with permission of the author.

Love Waltz With Fireworks
by Kelli Russell Agodon

Seventeen minutes ago, I was in love
    with the cashier and a cinnamon pull-apart,
    seven minutes before that, it was a gray-

haired man in argyle socks, a woman
  dancing outside the bakery holding
  a cigarette and broken umbrella. The rain,

I've fallen in love with it many times,
    the fog, the frost—how it covers the clovers
    —and by clovers I mean lovers.

things I see that I love (or feel)

And now I'm thinking how much I want to rush up
  to the stranger in the plaid wool hat
  and tell him how much I love his eyes,

all those fireworks, every seventeen minutes, exploding
  in my head—you the baker, you the novelist,
  you the reader, you the homeless man on the corner

what I wish I could say

with the strong hands—I've thought about you. But
in this world we've been taught to keep
    our emotions tight, a rubber band ball we worry

if one band loosens, the others will begin shooting off
  in so many directions. So we quiet.
    I quiet. I eat my cinnamon bread

in the bakery watching the old man still sitting
  at his table, moving his napkin as he drinks
  his small cup of coffee, and I never say,

...but how the world expects us to act

I think you're beautiful, except in my head,
except I decide I can't
  live this way, and walk over to him and

place my hand on his shoulder, lean in close
  and whisper, *I love your argyle socks,*
    and he grabs my hand,

the way a memory holds tight in the smallest
    corner. He smiles and says,
    I always hope someone will notice.

Instead, I decide to do

— his reaction

Acting On Impulse

things I see that make me feel/think/react	What I wish I could say	but how the world expects us to react	Instead, I decide to do/say	the reaction I get

A Walk

She loves walking
all the way around a jungle length of her neighborhood.

She grabs a leash and collar, just perfect for her dog
and heads out the door for a new adventure.

Now starting off,
a sunny day
before lunch and ready to eat.

She feels the wind blow through her hair,
not a single honk from her siblings.

With a long way to go,
a nice excited healthy dog to walk with,
it gives her energy and excitement.

She runs then walks,
catching her breath like her dog.
They're both hungry so they head back.

They're eating, but do not have the same good vibes.

She thinks you can still be happy
without the long walk.
She would think of the tweeting of the birds
and would be thankful for her dog.
She will never forget the feeling.

Audrie Soler
Grade 7

WRITE.

1 Freewrite for
3 minutes
(then set aside).

Think of a place outdoors and describe your senses there.

What might you see, hear, smell there?

*Nobody starts with a blank page.

READ.

Notice:
- use of white Space
- inventive (non-standard) use of parts of speech to create images
- the title names the place
- free verse

2 Read the poem.
Aloud. Slowly.
Read it again, and this time everyone should underline parts they find striking. Discuss the parts they notice. Name the craft. Notice the parts.

GET THE STRUCTURE.

3 Reveal the chunked poem. (Students copy the chunks.) Re-read the poem, watching the movement of the structure.

A Place (and its Sensory Details)

| what you see, smell, hear in that place | one thing you learned in that place | other sensory things that always happen there |

WRITE.

4 Invite students to write a poem.
Right now you have
- A page of thoughts
- Examples of craft you like
- A text structure

See what you come up with!
Use any of those, change any, and see what you write in the next minutes.

At the Lake
by Sarah Anderson

Above her thick white hair,
Birch leaves sun flicker,

The first time she taught me to break
a twig for the smell, I carried it for days.

She always pins her hair up
loosely. The lake water blinds us.

Source: "At the Lake" printed with permission of the author.

At the Lake
by Sarah Anderson

Above her thick white hair,
Birch leaves sun flicker,

— What I see, smell, hear in that place

The first time she taught me to break
a twig for the smell, I carried it for days.

— one thing I learned in that place

She always pins her hair up
loosely. The lake water blinds us.

other sensory things that happen here

A place (and its Sensory Details)

| what you see, smell, hear in that place | one thing you learned in that place | other sensory things that always happen there |

At the Beach

With her glazed, hazel eyes,
she saw a blinding ocean.

The first time they taught her
to gently walk into the waves.

She usually keeps a calm act,
but she was really excited.

**Alexis Ramirez
Grade 8**

The Garden

The flowers smell
so good like
candy.

I hear
the birds chirping.

I see my
friend Andy.

Andy knows
the life
cycle of a
butterfly.

**Sophia Gonzalez Cruz
Grade 5**

WRITE.

1 Freewrite for 3 minutes (then set aside).

> Who is one person you'd give the _best_ gift to?
>
> What all do you wish you could give them?

*Nobody starts with a blank page.

READ.

> Notice:
> • Simile
> • metaphor
> • repetition

2 Read the poem. Aloud. Slowly. Read it again, and this time everyone should underline parts they find striking. Discuss the parts they notice. Name the craft. Notice the parts.

GET THE STRUCTURE.

3 Reveal the chunked poem. (Students copy the chunks.) Re-read the poem, watching the movement of the structure.

> ## What I Give to You
>
> | what I offer you | what it is like | what else it is | what you can do with it | when you'll need it most |

WRITE.

4 Invite students to write a poem. Right now you have
- A page of thoughts
- Examples of craft you like
- A text structure

See what you come up with!
Use any of those, change any, and see what you write in the next minutes.

I Am Offering This Poem
by Jimmy Santiago Baca

I am offering this poem to you,
since I have nothing else to give.
Keep it like a warm coat
when winter comes to cover you,
or like a pair of thick socks
the cold cannot bite through,

I love you,

I have nothing else to give you,
so it is a pot full of yellow corn
to warm your belly in winter,
it is a scarf for your head, to wear
over your hair, to tie up around your face,

I love you,

Keep it, treasure this as you would
if you were lost, needing direction,
in the wilderness life becomes when mature;
and in the corner of your drawer,
tucked away like a cabin or hogan
in dense trees, come knocking,
and I will answer, give you directions,
and let you warm yourself by this fire,
rest by this fire, and make you feel safe

I love you,

It's all I have to give,
and all anyone needs to live,
and to go on living inside,
when the world outside
no longer cares if you live or die;
remember,

I love you.

Source: "I Am Offering This Poem" is reprinted with permission of the author.

I Am Offering This Poem
by Jimmy Santiago Baca

I am offering this poem to you,
since I have nothing else to give. — *What I offer you*
Keep it like a warm coat
when winter comes to cover you,
or like a pair of thick socks
the cold cannot bite through, — *what it is like*

I love you,

I have nothing else to give you,
so it is a pot full of yellow corn
to warm your belly in winter,
it is a scarf for your head, to wear
over your hair, to tie up around your face, — *What Else it is*

I love you,

Keep it, treasure this as you would
if you were lost, needing direction,
in the wilderness life becomes when mature;
and in the corner of your drawer,
tucked away like a cabin or hogan
in dense trees, come knocking,
and I will answer, give you directions,
and let you warm yourself by this fire,
rest by this fire, and make you feel safe — *ways you can use it*

I love you,

It's all I have to give,
and all anyone needs to live,
and to go on living inside,
when the world outside
no longer cares if you live or die;
remember, — *When you'll need it most*

I love you.

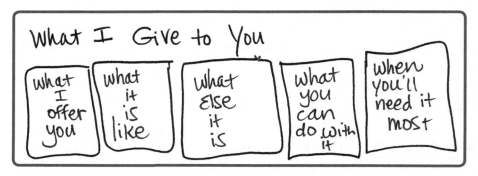

What I Give to You

| what I offer you | what it is like | what Else it is | what you can do with it | when you'll need it most |

Offering All I Can

Candy, perfume, dolls, maybe balloons

Nothing will do

Dolls—she would play with and get bored
Perfume—she would use and throw away
Balloons—she would let them float forever

Nothing will do

I cry for you
I beg for you
My smile, laugh, love
My gift is all for you

Nothing will do

Keep it love it
Make it yours
Carry it from 11 to always

Nothing will do

Then all I have to give is to let go
and love from a distance

When you are alone I will be behind
Don't forget

Harley Clark
Grade 8

WRITE.

1 Freewrite for 3 minutes (then set aside).

Who is someone you know with a quirky habit?

Or one unusual behavior?

Describe it.

*Nobody starts with a blank page.

READ.

Notice:
- the triple simile in the first part
- more similes
- the white space (for what effect)

2 Read the poem. Aloud. Slowly. Read it again, and this time everyone should underline parts they find striking. Discuss the parts they notice. Name the craft. Notice the parts.

GET THE STRUCTURE.

3 Reveal the chunked poem. (Students copy the chunks.) Re-read the poem, watching the movement of the structure.

Quirky Behavior

| the quirky thing they do | why they do it | what it makes me wonder | what they would answer |

WRITE.

4 Invite students to write a poem. Right now you have
- A page of thoughts
- Examples of craft you like
- A text structure

See what you come up with!
Use any of those, change any, and see what you write in the next minutes.

Possums
by Sheila Black

A kind of thrill—to lie on a road
and flatten yourself,

White fur like a ball of winter,

like the March blossoms on the fruit trees,
each one folded in like

the fledgling that never made it
from the nest.

They do this when they feel threatened,
Remain motionless

even when curious people come prod
them with sticks.

stiffening their pearly claws as a tree stiffens
its twigs for winter. What is it to be dead?

The possums know—that eternal watchfulness
by which the dead in their stately wisdom

watch us
who keep moving.

Source: "Possums," originally published on Poem-a-Day on February 7, 2017, by the Academy of American Poets, is reprinted with permission of the author.

4

Possums
by Sheila Black

A kind of thrill—to lie on a road
and flatten yourself,

White fur like a ball of winter,

like the March blossoms on the fruit trees,
each one folded in like

the fledgling that never made it
from the nest.

the Quirky thing they do

They do this when they feel threatened,
Remain motionless

even when curious people come prod
them with sticks.

why they do it

stiffening their pearly claws as a tree stiffens
its twigs for winter. What is it to be dead?

← *what it makes me wonder*

The possums know—that eternal watchfulness
by which the dead in their stately wisdom

What they would answer

watch us
who keep moving.

Quirky Behavior

| the quirky thing they do | why they do it | what it makes me wonder | what they would answer |

Quirky Behavior

What a thrill to gross everyone out.
It brings him joy to get people to go *eww*.
It surely wouldn't bring me joy.

Eyelids folded inward like a lizard.
Like someone reversed something backward
    in the wrong way.

Why does he do this?
We may never know.

Maybe he does it for fun like a sociopath.
Even when people tell him to stop,
he keeps going.

No matter what is going on, he keeps going.

Folding his eyelids inward and keeping a
    straight face.
What is it like to be like him?

He knows, staring at everybody, waiting for
    their next move.

Jackson Cline
Grade 7

The Whole Peanut

A great taste—
to not peel the shell and eat it whole.

Tan shell like the desert sand,
like the delivery boxes on the front porch
each one sturdy.

It's good as the yummy hot fudge sundae
that your mom made for you.

When I feel hungry, I eat the shell and all,
even when grossed out people
come and look at what I'm doing,
gagging as they watch me.

What is it like to eat the whole peanut?

I know. The eternal deliciousness
of eating the peanut with the shell.

Jacob Manasco
Grade 7

WRITE.

1 Freewrite for 3 minutes (then set aside).

> think about all the weird little things you remember from childhood (objects, places, truths)
>
> Describe as many as you can.

*Nobody starts with a blank page.

READ.

> Notice:
> • anaphora (repeated beginnings)
> • aside -pretty scary-
> • zooming in on uniqueness

2 Read the poem. Aloud. Slowly. Read it again, and this time everyone should underline parts they find striking. Discuss the parts they notice. Name the craft. Notice the parts.

GET THE STRUCTURE.

3 Reveal the chunked poem. (Students copy the chunks.) Re-read the poem, watching the movement of the structure.

> Memories Unique to You (List/Anaphora)
>
> | one weird thing I remember | another weird thing I remember | another weird thing I remember | ← repeat until you're done |

WRITE.

4 Invite students to write a poem. Right now you have
- A page of thoughts
- Examples of craft you like
- A text structure

See what you come up with!
Use any of those, change any, and see what you write in the next minutes.

I Remember (Excerpt)
by Joe Brainard

I remember that the only friends my parents had who owned a swimming pool also owned a funeral parlor.

I remember laundromats at night all lit up with nobody in them.

I remember a very clean Catholic book-gift shop with practically nothing in it to buy.

I remember rearranging boxes of candy so it would look like not so much was missing.

I remember brown and white shoes with little decorative holes cut out of them.

I remember certain group gatherings that are hard to get up and leave from.

I remember alligators and quicksand in jungle movies. (Pretty scary.)

I remember opening jars that nobody else could open.

I remember making home-made ice cream.

I remember that I liked store-bought ice cream better.

I remember hospital supply store windows.

I remember stories of what hot dogs are made of.

I remember Davy Crockett hats. And Davy Crockett just about everything else.

I remember not understanding why people on the other side of the world didn't fall off.

I Remember (Excerpt)
by Joe Brainard

I remember that the only friends my parents had who owned a swimming pool also owned a funeral parlor.

I remember laundromats at night all lit up with nobody in them.

I remember a very clean Catholic book-gift shop with practically nothing in it to buy.

I remember rearranging boxes of candy so it would look like not so much was missing.

I remember brown and white shoes with little decorative holes cut out of them.

I remember certain group gatherings that are hard to get up and leave from.

I remember alligators and quicksand in jungle movies. (Pretty scary.)

I remember opening jars that nobody else could open.

I remember making home-made ice cream.

I remember that I liked store-bought ice cream better.

I remember hospital supply store windows.

I remember stories of what hot dogs are made of.

I remember Davy Crockett hats. And Davy Crockett just about everything else.

I remember not understanding why people on the other side of the world didn't fall off.

weird things I remember

Memories Unique to You (List/Anaphora)

| one weird thing I remember | another weird thing I remember | another weird thing I remember | ← repeat until you're done |

22

I Remember

I remember my parents had no friends when we first moved to Texas.
I remember going to school with everything that was new.
I remember playing with my dog Max and eating junk food with him.
I remember learning English for the first time.
I remember when I first saw my new house (very big).
I remember going to the park with my twin sister.
I remember playing hide-and-seek with my neighbors.
I remember eating chocolates all day.
I remember turning 5 on my birthday.
I remember going to kindergarten on the first day of school.
I remember having new friends.
I remember having play dates with my besties.
I remember not understanding my teacher, because she spoke English.

Aymun Memon
Grade 5

I Remember

I remember that when we baked cookies I would sit in front of the oven and watch them bake.
I remember we celebrated the 100th day of school in elementary school.
I remember pretending to be an orphan and my sister was my adoption mother.
I remember waking up from eye surgery and my sisters helping me.
I remember sledding down a steep hill and flipping over.
I remember Christmas mornings how happy I would be.
I remember going to Disneyland for the first time and thinking about how magical it was.
I remember zip lining in Costa Rica and watching the horses from 650 ft. in the air.
I remember when my dad came home from work, I would give him running hugs.
I remember swimming in the hot tub while it was snowing in the winter.
I remember when I first got glasses and actually being able to see the world around me.
I remember flying on a plane for the first time going to New Mexico.
I remember watching the fireworks on the 4th of July without neighbors.
I remember having lemonade stands and making over 100 dollars.
I remember finishing my first year of middle school and being glad it was over.

Ivy Clyne
Grade 6

WRITE.

1 Freewrite for 3 minutes (then set aside).

Think about some kind of food in your family, one thing someone makes -- that you really like to eat.

Write about that.

*Nobody starts with a blank page.

READ.

Notice:
- the importance of the verbs
- perspective changing
- crisp language
- Simile
- metaphor

2 Read the poem. Aloud. Slowly. Read it again, and this time everyone should underline parts they find striking. Discuss the parts they notice. Name the craft. Notice the parts.

GET THE STRUCTURE.

3 Reveal the chunked poem. (Students copy the chunks.) Re-read the poem, watching the movement of the structure.

Watching Someone Do Something

| what they are doing as you watch | what you see when you shift your gaze to the outside | what new thing you see when you look at the person now | a question about a change coming in your future |

WRITE.

4 Invite students to write a poem.
Right now you have
- A page of thoughts
- Examples of craft you like
- A text structure

See what you come up with!
Use any of those, change any, and see what you write in the next minutes.

My Mother's Tortilla
by Joanne Diaz

She slices each potato thin enough

to see the light pass through its flesh. The oil

in the skillet heats until its scent

rises in a spool of smoke. I watch

her knuckles as she grasps the spatula,

pours the beaten eggs over each slice,

then, later, sweeps along the oily edge

as the tortilla blossoms in the pan.

Beyond her, the kitchen's heat dissolves

the latticework of frost that webs each pane

of glass. The branches crisp beneath the ice;

we hear the crackle, wait until their fall.

My mother inhales deeply, leans her hip

into the oven's edge. She refuses help,

the flesh of her waving like a curtain

after a long play. A few strong bones

hold her in one place—the rest are like

light spirits, growing rare and thin.

How long until she vanishes, until

the pinkish-white of each bone's glow becomes

Venetian glass, then chipped mosaic, then

dust that rises from Assyrian walls? Her spine

marks the question; she offers me a slice.

Source: "My Mother's Tortilla" is reprinted with permission of Silverfish Review Press, publisher and copyright holder of *The Lessons*.

My Mother's Tortilla
by Joanne Diaz

She slices each potato thin enough
to see the light pass through its flesh. The oil
in the skillet heats until its scent
rises in a spool of smoke. I watch
her knuckles as she grasps the spatula,
pours the beaten eggs over each slice,
then, later, sweeps along the oily edge
as the tortilla blossoms in the pan.

what she is doing as I watch

Beyond her, the kitchen's heat dissolves
the latticework of frost that webs each pane
of glass. The branches crisp beneath the ice;
we hear the crackle, wait until their fall.

what is happening outside

My mother inhales deeply, leans her hip
into the oven's edge. She refuses help,
the flesh of her waving like a curtain
after a long play. A few strong bones
hold her in one place—the rest are like
light spirits, growing rare and thin.

Something new I notice when I look at her again

How long until she vanishes, until
the pinkish-white of each bone's glow becomes
Venetian glass, then chipped mosaic, then
dust that rises from Assyrian walls? Her spine
marks the question; she offers me a slice.

a question about a change coming in the future

Watching Someone Do Something

| *what they are doing as you watch* | *what you see when you shift your gaze to the outside* | *what new thing you see when you look at the person now* | *a question about a change coming in your future* |

Moments to Cherish

I watch my mom as she makes chicken and dumplings.
She carefully cuts the chicken into tiny slivers
and throws them into the giant pot on the stove.
I hear the boiling water bubble, and look outside, see
a mama blue jay returning to her nest.
She has brought back food for her tiny baby bird.
A mother taking care of her young,
just as my mom is doing for me.
I look at my mom,
see the joy in her eyes as she teaches me how to cook.
How many more moments will we spend together
when I start college
or inevitably move out?
I don't know the answer, so I cherish
this moment as though it is the last.

Brooke Kalinec
Grade 12

Thanksgiving

My mom gets the turkey
and puts it on the table. I remember
two years ago I put an orange in
the turkey and it turned into jelly
when we cooked it. I help my mom
get the ingredients out. I turn to see
my aunt peeling potatoes, my sister
getting the beans, and my brother pouring
rice in the bowl. My dad and uncle go get
the BBQ meat and the lighters. When I see
my mom, she has a sad face, looking depressed.
I have no idea what it is, but she is sad.
Maybe because she hasn't seen her father
and brothers for Thanksgiving. I wonder
if I'll ever see my mom's family
and I hope they are nice.

Jesse Briones
Grade 6

WRITE.

1 Freewrite for 3 minutes (then set aside).

Think of someone you were with, and together you went some place, and you have a special memory of it.

Spend a few minutes writing about that time, and that place.

*Nobody starts with a blank page.

READ.

Notice:
- parenthetical voice -- younger, or older
- repetition
- rhythm

2 Read the poem. Aloud. Slowly.
Read it again, and this time everyone should underline parts they find striking. Discuss the parts they notice. Name the craft. Notice the parts.

GET THE STRUCTURE.

3 Reveal the chunked poem. (Students copy the chunks.) Re-read the poem, watching the movement of the structure.

A Usual (Unusual) Memory

| the place I remember | What we did there | what I knew at that moment | how the moment felt to me |

WRITE.

4 Invite students to write a poem.
Right now you have
- A page of thoughts
- Examples of craft you like
- A text structure

See what you come up with!
Use any of those, change any, and see what you write in the next minutes.

Still Life With Summer Sausage, a Blade, and No Blood
by Vievee Francis

East Texas, 198__

I remember, we walked (we didn't walk)
from the farmhouse to the store in Palestine
(we drove the truck, got out, went in).
The storefronts hadn't changed since
my father was a child. He grabbed saltines from the bin
(he bought a box) and he bought some sausage.
We walked (yes, by then we walked) around town
as we ate (he shared). He gave me some summer
sausage, cut with his pocket knife. I pulled the pieces
from the point of the blade. I knew (knew)
nothing would happen (though he was silent)
to alter his memory. We were together
in Texas and we ate and walked in silence
and it felt like smiling, like skipping, like saying,
"Daddy" and him not minding, not minding at all.

Source: Francis, Vievee. "Still Life With Summer Sausage, a Blade, and No Blood," from *Horse in the Dark*, Evanston, IN: Northwestern University Press, 2012. p. 69. Copyright © 2012 by Vievee Francis. Published 2012 by Northwestern University Press.

**Still Life With Summer Sausage, a Blade, and No Blood
by Vievee Francis**

East Texas, 198—

I remember, we walked (we didn't walk)
from the farmhouse to the store in Palestine
(we drove the truck, got out, went in).
The storefronts hadn't changed since
my father was a child. He grabbed saltines from the bin
(he bought a box) and he bought some sausage.
We walked (yes, by then we walked) around town
as we ate (he shared). He gave me some summer
sausage, cut with his pocket knife. I pulled the pieces
from the point of the blade. I knew (knew)
nothing would happen (though he was silent)
to alter his memory. We were together
in Texas and we ate and walked in silence
and it felt like smiling, like skipping, like saying,
"Daddy" and him not minding, not minding at all.

a place I remember

what we did there

what I knew at that moment

how that moment felt

A Usual (Unusual) Memory

| the place I remember | what we did there | what I knew at that moment | how the moment felt to me |

I Remember

I remember
Going below the dam
Walking the 3-mile trail
With my mom
Thinking maybe
Our relationship would be better.
But instead of talking
All there was
Was silence (It felt like I was drowning in silence,
    thick like syrup)
After our walk
I went
To the basketball court (Mom went on the
    trail again)
To keep my ripstick rolling
I fell into a rhythm
With my legs (Back and forth, Back and forth)
Getting swallowed
By my favorite songs
I hadn't realized
Darkness was falling
Until my legs
Screamed of exhaustion (My mom still hadn't
    finished the trail yet)
On wobbly legs
I walked
To the merry-go-round
Staring off into space
I waited
Gently
I pushed myself
Around
With my foot (ring-around-the-rosie)
Finally
Just as the moon shone bright
I saw my mother
Walking towards me
A look on her face. (Ashes, ashes, we all fall down)
Just then
Three words
Came out
Of her mouth
"I love you" (and my walls came crumbling down)

Aaliyah Walls
Grade 7

Woodlawn (Jorge) Park

I remember we walked for miles
(a couple maybe) 'til we reached
this beautiful tree with a lake
at its roots. As we sat in the grass
watching the sun setting (very
quickly) with the traffic rolling
across the way (only a few meters)
a car (actually a white truck) drove by
with its radio blaring. A song I like.
I knew in that moment that I had
fallen in love, not only with him
but with the memory we just made.
As I sank deeply into his arms, I knew
as much as I wanted this to last,
it wouldn't (at least not forever).
On my first date with my first
boyfriend, I fell in love with everything,
because everything felt so bliss.

Kayla Upton
Grade 10

WRITE.

1 Freewrite for 3 minutes (then set aside).

Describe something you were required to do,

Something you didn't want to do.

*Nobody starts with a blank page.

READ.

Notice:
- Simile
- Speech in italics
- images

2 Read the poem. Aloud. Slowly. Read it again, and this time everyone should underline parts they find striking. Discuss the parts they notice. Name the craft. Notice the parts.

GET THE STRUCTURE.

3 Reveal the chunked poem. (Students copy the chunks.) Re-read the poem, watching the movement of the structure.

Flashback to Drudgery

| Something you were required to do | What the person in charge did or said | Your favorite adult-in-charge (what they looked like, would do or say) | how it Ended |

WRITE.

4 Invite students to write a poem. Right now you have
- A page of thoughts
- Examples of craft you like
- A text structure

See what you come up with!
Use any of those, change any, and see what you write in the next minutes.

Chorus, Venable Elementary
by Ann Hudson

Mrs. King would drag her pick across that autoharp
like she was stripping paint, and work with us through our songs
for the Christmas Concert, even though it was still a warm
October afternoon, the huge casement windows opened a few inches
for the breeze off the playground, where the older kids
were out for recess already. By December, we'd beaten
Those songs to death, but not learned them any better,
and every year there'd be a day Mrs. King would weep
by the piano. *The concert is in four days. Four days!*
and then Mrs. Clements would come in and put her arm
around Mrs. King's shoulders, and call her *Rosie.*
Mrs. C would wink at us, and we'd do our best to sing.
I liked Mrs. King just fine, but still felt loyal to the teacher
I'd had in kindergarten. She bewitched us all, so tall
and willowy. She'd sit, not cross-legged on the carpeted floor,
but with her long, coltish legs tucked to one side, ankles crossed,
Her hair so brown and shimmery, was long enough
she could sit on it as she played the bells, the clear notes
ringing out. No one was more beautiful. Apparently,
the married principal agreed, because by June
they'd run off together to Hawaii. I knew I'd hate his guts forever.

Source: "Chorus, Venable Elementary" is printed with permission of the author.

8 TEXT STRUCTURE

From "Chorus, Venable Elementary"

Chorus, Venable Elementary
by Ann Hudson

Mrs. King would drag her pick across that autoharp
like she was stripping paint, and work with us through our songs
for the Christmas Concert, even though it was still a warm
October afternoon, the huge casement windows opened a few inches
for the breeze off the playground, where the older kids
were out for recess already. By December, we'd beaten
Those songs to death, but not learned them any better,
and every year there'd be a day Mrs. King would weep
by the piano. *The concert is in four days. Four days!*
and then Mrs. Clements would come in and put her arm
around Mrs. King's shoulders, and call her *Rosie.*
Mrs. C would wink at us, and we'd do our best to sing.
I liked Mrs. King just fine, but still felt loyal to the teacher
I'd had in kindergarten. She bewitched us all, so tall
and willowy. She'd sit, not cross-legged on the carpeted floor,
but with her long, coltish legs tucked to one side, ankles crossed.
Her hair so brown and shimmery, was long enough
she could sit on it as she played the bells, the clear notes
ringing out. No one was more beautiful. Apparently,
the married principal agreed, because by June
they'd run off together to Hawaii. I knew I'd hate his guts forever.

what I was required to do

what the person in charge did or said

my favorite adult-in charge, and what they would do/say/look like

how it ended

Flashback to Drudgery
Something you were required to do
what the person in charge did or said
your favorite adult-in-charge (what they looked like, would do or say)
how it Ended

The Dread

My mother told me to do it,
go up and see my grandfather who had recently passed.
It took mountains of courage to go up,
but when I did, I crumbled
and the only thing I wanted was to go home and cry.
I ran to the lounge, plunged down
on a couch. My mother came up and said:
we're going through this together.
It broke my heart even more
when we had to go and clean out his house.
My hogging relatives took everything,
but I took home the things that my grandfather gave to me.
I cherish those things, especially the Corvette models.
He was always working on Corvettes,
and every time I see one, I feel like I'm right back
in his garage, looking between him and his '72 Corvette.
Now we are selling his house
and it's very sad. We can't afford
to keep it, and it's hard to see it go.

Charlie Fronick
Grade 7

WRITE.

1 Freewrite for 3 minutes (then set aside).

Describe an Element of the weather in a place you Know Well.

*Nobody starts with a blank page.

READ.

Notice:
- Sound words
- dialogue
  written without quotation marks
- Specific names

2 Read the poem. Aloud. Slowly.
Read it again, and this time everyone should underline parts they find striking. Discuss the parts they notice. Name the craft. Notice the parts.

GET THE STRUCTURE.

3 Reveal the chunked poem. (Students copy the chunks.) Re-read the poem, watching the movement of the structure.

Weather Around Us

| what the weather touches | What all the people are doing | what the weather continues to do | Voices (what the people are saying) | last voice about the weather |

WRITE.

4 Invite students to write a poem.
Right now you have
- A page of thoughts
- Examples of craft you like
- A text structure

See what you come up with!
Use any of those, change any, and see what you write in the next minutes.

Snow in North Jersey
by August Kleinzahler

Snow is falling along the Boulevard

and its little cemeteries hugged by transmission shops

and on the stone bear in the park

and the WWI monument, making a crust

on the soldier with his chin strap and bayonet

It's blowing in from the west

over the low hills and meadowlands

swirling past the giant cracking stills

that flare all night along the Turnpike

It is with a terrible deliberateness

that Mr. Ruiz reaches into his back pocket

and counts out $18 and change for his Lotto picks

while in the upstairs of a thousand duplexes

with the TV on, cancers tick   tick   tick

and the snow continues to fall and blanket

these crowded rows of frame and brick

with their heartbreaking castellations

and the red '68 Impala on blocks

and Joe he's drinking again and Myra's boy Tommy

in the old days it would have been a disgrace

and Father Keenan's not been having a good winter

and it was nice enough this morning

till noon anyhow with the sun sitting up there like a crown

over a great big dome of mackerel sky

But it's coming down now all right...

Snow in North Jersey
by August Kleinzahler

Snow is falling along the Boulevard
and its little cemeteries hugged by transmission shops
and on the stone bear in the park
and the WWI monument, making a crust
on the soldier with his chin strap and bayonet
It's blowing in from the west
over the low hills and meadowlands
swirling past the giant cracking stills
that flare all night along the Turnpike

what the weather touches

It is with a terrible deliberateness
that Mr. Ruiz reaches into his back pocket
and counts out $18 and change for his Lotto picks
while in the upstairs of a thousand duplexes
with the TV on, cancers tick   tick   tick

what the people are doing

and the snow continues to fall and blanket
these crowded rows of frame and brick
with their heartbreaking castellations
and the red '68 Impala on blocks

continuation... back to the weather

and Joe he's drinking again and Myra's boy Tommy
in the old days it would have been a disgrace
and Father Keenan's not been having a good winter
and it was nice enough this morning
till noon anyhow with the sun sitting up there like a crown
over a great big dome of mackerel sky

what people are saying

But it's coming down now all right...

final voice

Weather Around Us

what the weather touches	what all the people are doing	what the weather continues to do	Voices (what the people are saying)	last voice about the weather

Rain in Olmos Park

The clouds are crying down on the newly-
   paved streets
and the perfectly manicured lawns with flowers of
   every color,
on the small toddlers wearing red rain boots
on the smooth, gray track that seems to
   go on forever,
challenging people to exercise.
The rain comes from the north,
over endless fields with innocent cows and
riots over absurd politicians and their vicious lies.
It's with a great sadness
that Ms. Gray cancels her plans
to have a picnic in the always-vacant
park down the street,
while across the lawn the kids
embrace the rain and spin in circles.
The clouds continue to weep on the happy plants
and the ancient pecan tree with thousands of leaves
and Mrs. and Mr. Smith arguing on their front porch
   about nothing
but the rain slows and eventually stops.

Emily Bond
Grade 8

No Snow, Just Heat

During this time
you think it is cold
but no cold
no snow
just heat.
Here on Delgado Street
it's very hot.
You can see my neighbor
getting beers for all his friends
and my little baby cousin Matthew getting ice cream
from the freezer. You can see
how tired people are because they come home all
   full of sweat
and they are very thirsty from the heat.
People are dehydrated.
My grandma goes and gets water for us
and then finally it gets dark.

Isabella Rodriguez
Grade 6

WRITE.

1 Freewrite for 3 minutes (then set aside).

Think of a time you were trying to do something but it wasn't any fun until someone joined in.
Write about that.

*Nobody starts with a blank page.

READ.

Notice:
- narrative
- persona/voice
- repetition
- rhythm
- tone

2 Read the poem. Aloud. Slowly. Read it again, and this time everyone should underline parts they find striking. Discuss the parts they notice. Name the craft. Notice the parts.

GET THE STRUCTURE.

3 Reveal the chunked poem. (Students copy the chunks.) Re-read the poem, watching the movement of the structure.

Side by Side

| What you were trying to do | why it didn't work | advice you got | who joined in | what doesn't last | what does last |

WRITE.

4 Invite students to write a poem. Right now you have
- A page of thoughts
- Examples of craft you like
- A text structure

See what you come up with!
Use any of those, change any, and see what you write in the next minutes.

Draw
by Amy Ludwig VanDerwater

Cavemom said, *draw on our walls!*
Caveboy got a bone
dipped it into mud and blood.
And then he felt alone.

The wall was blank. The wall was clear.
He stood in place. He stared in fear.
How would he fill this empty space?
Cavemom looked into his face.

Caveboy darling. Caveboy child.
Draw the bison, free and wild.
Draw your father.
Draw a deer.
Draw your life.
Draw right here.

He drew one tree. She drew another.
They drew all morning, boy and mother.

Someday
we will all be gone.
But art we make lives on and on.

Draw
by Amy Ludwig VanDerwater

Cavemom said, *draw on our walls!*
Caveboy got a bone
dipped it into mud and blood.
And then he felt alone.

what he was trying to do

The wall was blank. The wall was clear.
He stood in place. He stared in fear.
How would he fill this empty space?
Cavemom looked into his face.

why it didn't work

Caveboy darling. Caveboy child.
Draw the bison, free and wild.
Draw your father.
Draw a deer.
Draw your life.
Draw right here.

what the mom advised

He drew one tree. She drew another.
They drew all morning, boy and mother.

she joined in

Someday
we will all be gone.
But art we make lives on and on.

we won't last forever
our art will

Side by Side

| What you were trying to do | why it didn't work | advice you got | Who joined in | what doesn't last | what does last |

Seven Little Raindrops

A little drop of water
Floating in the sky
He felt himself getting stronger
But kept on floating by and by

He was full and he was heavy
He wanted to stay in the blue above
To leave home, he was not ready
But knew his time was to come

He moped and he wallowed
Afraid of being alone
His friends heard him and soon followed
And they fell through the ozone

Flying through the heaven
Plummeting to earth
The little raindrops, all seven
Fell to the ground, but full of mirth

They are no longer here
But their laughter still echoes
And even though they disappear
They have watered all the meadows

Jana Jarvis
College Student

WRITE.

1 Freewrite for 3 minutes (then set aside).

Look at some Hopper paintings, printed or online. Choose a painting you like. Imagine you're one of the people. Write for a couple of minutes.

*Nobody starts with a blank page.

READ.

Notice:
- Poetic form EKPHRASTIC poem (poem about a painting or song)
- running dialogue
- metaphor

2 Read the poem. Aloud. Slowly.
Read it again, and this time everyone should underline parts they find striking. Discuss the parts they notice. Name the craft. Notice the parts.

GET THE STRUCTURE.

3 Reveal the chunked poem. (Students copy the chunks.) Re-read the poem, watching the movement of the structure.

Interpersonal Dynamics (Ekphrastic)

| one person and what they are doing | What/who that person reminds me of and why | Who I am in the painting and what I want | Something this makes me wonder about the other person's life | what is stopping me | a question about another detail in the painting |

WRITE.

4 Invite students to write a poem.
Right now you have
- A page of thoughts
- Examples of craft you like
- A text structure

See what you come up with!
Use any of those, change any, and see what you write in the next minutes.

Nighthawks by Edward Hopper
by Nathan McClain

See how closely she sits to the man
in the blue suit? See how their hands
almost touch? How she reminds me
of my mother—a woman in red

drinking coffee. See?
Hopper was obviously lonely.
Why else would he paint her, my mother,
sitting there like this?

Which would make me what?
The soda jerk in white?
I'm eager enough. I want to help.
Even if it means simply waiting

to light each man's cigarette.
My mother spent
nights alone, wiping coffee mugs
clean of dust. How the lines

that creased her mouth deepened…
See? And what if she dies
this way—sad, untouched?
I say I want to help

but it's as if my voice is a faucet
running—a refrigerator's empty hum

Hopper was obviously lonely.
Why else paint the gray-suited man
at the counter, my father, his back turned?

Source: "Nighthawks by Edward Hopper" from *Scale* (2017) by Nathan McClain. Printed with permission of Four Way Books.
All rights reserved.

Nighthawks by Edward Hopper
by Nathan McClain

See how closely she sits to the man
in the blue suit? See how their hands
almost touch? How she reminds me
of my mother—a woman in red

drinking coffee. See?
Hopper was obviously lonely.
Why else would he paint her, my mother,
sitting there like this?

*one person
you see*

*Who it
reminds
you of*

Which would make me what?
The soda jerk in white?
I'm eager enough. I want to help.
Even if it means simply waiting

to light each man's cigarette.

*Who I am
in the painting
and
what I want*

My mother spent
nights alone, wiping coffee mugs
clean of dust. How the lines

that creased her mouth deepened...
See? And what if she dies
this way—sad, untouched?
I say I want to help

*What this
makes me
wonder
about that
other person*

but it's as if my voice is a faucet
running—a refrigerator's empty hum

*What is
stopping
me*

Hopper was obviously lonely.
Why else paint the gray-suited man
at the counter, my father, his back turned?

*a question
about another
detail in the painting*

Interpersonal Dynamics (Ekphrastic)

one person and what they are doing	What/who that person reminds me of and why	Who I am in the painting and what I want	Something this makes me wonder about the other person's life	what is stopping me	a question about another detail in the painting

The Scream (in response to Edvard Munch's *The Scream*)

There's no one in sight,
I've been running for millennia and dynasties,
for decades, years, minutes and seconds,
and everything in between.

I started screaming on day 26.
And I can't seem to stop.

Nobody sees me,
nobody cares for the sorrow in my scream,
or how I want this road to END.

I pass people with
Smiles and families with love and
peace.
The sweet, quiet, peace
I long for, but these feet can't make the trip.
I fall.

I started screaming on day 26,
It's day 12,936,757

One day I will see peace, and quiet.
And finally it will be the end.

Liliana Ramirez
Grade 6

Automat (after Edward Hopper)

Do you see the woman
who drinks her coffee
so quietly? She reminds me
of an old friend.

Do you see how she sits
with the roses next to her?
Like she's waiting for someone
to talk to her.

But I'm just the woman
Who sits uselessly in the back.
Red hair in a bandana,
I'm like a poster girl.

I want to help,
even if it's something small.
But she won't try
to even look at me.

It makes me wonder
if my nightly greetings
ever make her bitter days
even a little sweeter?

Lola Suffridge
Grade 6

WRITE.

1

Freewrite for
3 minutes
(then set aside).

> Describe a few
> places that you
> normally go to,
> places that have
> different rules for
> behavior.
> Write about what's
> normal in those places.

*Nobody starts with a blank page.

READ.

> Notice :
> • unrhymed verse
> • hypothetical
>   question
>   (disrupts the
>   thought)
> • rich visual
>   detail

2

Read the poem.
Aloud. Slowly.
Read it again, and this
time everyone should underline
parts they find striking. Discuss
the parts they notice. Name the
craft. Notice the parts.

GET THE STRUCTURE.

3

Reveal the chunked poem. (Students copy
the chunks.) Re-read the poem, watching
the movement of the structure.

> Unwritten Rules for Where I Am
>
> | how people behave in this place | Examples of what they do | a different place, and something that signals different rules | What I notice about this place I'm in |

WRITE.

4

Invite students to write a poem.
Right now you have

• A page of thoughts
• Examples of craft you like
• A text structure

See what you come up with!
Use any of those, change any, and see what you write
in the next minutes.

Full Capacity
by Rose McLarney

It's called a *kneeling bus* because it lowers for those who need it.
And we bend our knees to allow others to pass. Here,
we're humble. The woman holding her briefcase the whole time
so it won't slip onto my side, the man mouthing every word
he reads but careful not to make a sound, each person
trying to fit some task into the bounds of their small seat
and hour, all diligence, drawn elbows, and dropped eyes.
There is not enough room to unfold the newspaper's
black headline ("Habitat Destruction"), but somehow, hope fits.
The others too, headed home, must look out the window
when we pass a building with a balloon tied to the mailbox.
Imagine that was your welcome. *You are wanted here.*
How often can humans feel less than harmful to where we are?
Balloons just outline the space occupied by the air
we would have expelled anyway, but they fill a room
with the promise of cake, sugar paste connecting one layer
to more of itself. Bus riders stack on board,
scanning for seats. There are open spaces, if only
in our searching eyes.

Source: "Full Capacity" first appeared in *The Southern Review* and is reprinted with permission of the author.

Full Capacity
by Rose McLarney

It's called a *kneeling bus* because it lowers for those who need it.
And we bend our knees to allow others to pass. Here,
we're humble. The woman holding her briefcase the whole time
so it won't slip onto my side, the man mouthing every word
he reads but careful not to make a sound, each person
trying to fit some task into the bounds of their small seat
and hour, all diligence, drawn elbows, and dropped eyes.
There is not enough room to unfold the newspaper's
black headline ("Habitat Destruction"), but somehow, hope fits.

The others too, headed home, must look out the window
when we pass a building with a balloon tied to the mailbox.
Imagine that was your welcome. *You are wanted here.*
How often can humans feel less than harmful to where we are?
Balloons just outline the space occupied by the air
we would have expelled anyway, but they fill a room
with the promise of cake, sugar paste connecting one layer
to more of itself. Bus riders stack on board,
scanning for seats. There are open spaces, if only
in our searching eyes.

how people behave in this place

examples of what they do

a different place and something that signals different rules

What I notice about the place I'm in

Unwritten Rules for Where I Am

| *how people behave in this place* | *Examples of what they do* | *a different place, and something that signals different rules* | *What I notice about this place I'm in* |

In the Cell Phone World

We never look up to talk to each other.
We look at our world through our phones, not our eyes.
Crowds of people are glued to their devices
like flies on a sticky trap.

It doesn't matter, rich or poor,
everyone has a phone. It's more important
than food or water or a roof over our heads.
If we look up, it's only for a photo
or to count the likes it will get.

Like a genie in a bottle,
it can grant our wishes, yet
we become prisoners of our device.

There are places where there's no
cell tower in sight. People don't use
their phone to answer their questions.
The roots of humanity remain planted.

I live in a world
where society accepts the chaos
of technology expanding. We don't see
the simple beauty that our ancestors once saw.

Sofia Anahi Rodriguez
Grade 10

TEACHING NOTES
for "Because of Libraries We Can Say These Things"

WRITE.

1 Freewrite for 3 minutes (then set aside).

> People feel free when they are doing something they most love to do. They lose track of time and forget ordinary things for a while. What do you do that gives you that feeling?

*Nobody starts with a blank page.

READ.

> Notice:
> • free verse
> • 3rd person point of view
> • Ending image has ambiguous multiple meanings

2 Read the poem. Aloud. Slowly. Read it again, and this time everyone should underline parts they find striking. Discuss the parts they notice. Name the craft. Notice the parts.

GET THE STRUCTURE.

3 Reveal the chunked poem. (Students copy the chunks.) Re-read the poem, watching the movement of the structure.

> The Thing I Love to Do
>
> | what you have to do before you do the thing | When you get to do the thing | how it feels | what the thing can give you | how to keep the magic when life becomes ordinary |

WRITE.

4 Invite students to write a poem. Right now you have
- A page of thoughts
- Examples of craft you like
- A text structure

See what you come up with!
Use any of those, change any, and see what you write in the next minutes.

Because of Libraries We Can Say These Things
by Naomi Shihab Nye

She is holding the book close to her body,
carrying it home on the cracked sidewalk,
down the tangled hill.
If a dog runs at her again, she will use the book as a shield.

She looked hard among the long lines
of books to find this one.
When they start talking about money,
when the day contains such long and hot places,
she will go inside.
An orange bed is waiting.
Story without corners.
She will have two families.
They will eat at different hours.

She is carrying a book past the fire station
and the five and dime.

What this town has not given her
the book will provide; a sheep,
a wilderness of new solutions.
The book has already lived through its troubles.
The book has a calm cover, a straight spine.

When the step returns to itself,
as the best place for sitting,
and the old men up and down the street
are latching their clippers,

she will not be alone.
She will have a book to open
and open and open.
Her life starts here.

Source: Naomi Shihab Nye, "Because of Libraries We Can Say These Things" from *Fuel*. Copyright © 1998 by Naomi Shihab Nye. Used with the permission of The Permissions Company, LLC on behalf of BOA Editions, Ltd., www.boaeditions.org.

Because of Libraries We Can Say These Things
by Naomi Shihab Nye

what she does before she can read

She is holding the book close to her body,
carrying it home on the cracked sidewalk,
down the tangled hill.
If a dog runs at her again, she will use the book as a shield.

She looked hard among the long lines
of books to find this one.

when she gets to read

When they start talking about money,
when the day contains such long and hot places,
she will go inside.

how it feels

An orange bed is waiting.
Story without corners.
She will have two families.
They will eat at different hours.

what the book offers her

She is carrying a book past the fire station
and the five and dime.

What this town has not given her
the book will provide; a sheep,
a wilderness of new solutions.
The book has already lived through its troubles.
The book has a calm cover, a straight spine.

how to keep the magic

When the step returns to itself,
as the best place for sitting,
and the old men up and down the street
are latching their clippers,

she will not be alone.
She will have a book to open
and open and open.
Her life starts here.

---

the thing I love to Do

| what you have to do before you do the thing | when you get to do the thing | how it feels | what the thing can give you | how to keep the magic when life becomes ordinary |

Leap of Faith

She is standing, her legs trembling
desperately wanting to jump into
the still blue water.
People were laughing
but me, I was scared to take a big leap.

Then I jump.
SPLASH!
The water is ice cold on my skin.
It engulfs me, but I don't fight it,
because it's a wave of relief from the
    blazing hot sun.

All of my worries are swept away.
The pool gives me a sense of flying,
    calmness, and peace.
It makes the stress of the day melt away
like an ice cube on the hot pavement.

When I stand at the edge
of the high dive now, I think:
How did I do this in the first place?

But I have the courage
To take the leap.

Bella Nasis
Grade 7

For "Because of Libraries ..."

Stale and lonely
and wondering why

I leave the house
drive down Broadway by the
long-familiar houses with lush yards.
The McNay Art Museum smiles
at me and I run to the
Old Masters section.

Cobalt and comfort embrace me in
Monet's water lilies,
the Van Gogh ladies nod at me.

That timeless mansion is soothing and
permanent.
I'll certainly need it again.

Sandra Boydston
Adult Writer

WRITE.

1 Freewrite for 3 minutes (then set aside).

Think of something (not human) that's really interesting to you.
Think about what you would say to that object.

*Nobody starts with a blank page.

READ.

Notice:
- Poetic form EPISTOLARY poem (written in letter form)
- direct address
- point of view
- similes
- metaphors
- truism/life lesson

2 Read the poem. Aloud. Slowly.
Read it again, and this time everyone should underline parts they find striking. Discuss the parts they notice. Name the craft. Notice the parts.

GET THE STRUCTURE.

3 Reveal the chunked poem. (Students copy the chunks.) Re-read the poem, watching the movement of the structure.

11- Minute Poem

real life example → truism → literary example → how it relates to me today → Question about the truism

WRITE.

4 Invite students to write a poem. Right now you have
- A page of thoughts
- Examples of craft you like
- A text structure

See what you come up with!
Use any of those, change any, and see what you write in the next minutes.

Letter to a Cockroach, Now Dead and Mixed Into a Bar of Chocolate
by Matthew Olzmann

Regulations allow for, on average, sixty insect fragments
per hundred grams of chocolate
in America. You are pulverized.
The thorax, the head, the legs that no longer twitch.
Invisible and milk-smooth.
Nothing harbors a secret like sweetness.

Centuries ago, the Sirens understood
this statute. Each sank their knowledge
inside a voice of chimes and kisses,
hiding the ocean's stone teeth
in a mouth of mist and foam.

Yesterday, waves beat against a dock in Brazil.
The quick bodies of you and your buddies
quivered across the cargo of cacao beans.
You couldn't possibly comprehend: the beans
on their way to the grinder, just as those ancient sailors
couldn't envision—beyond the Sirens' music—
the broken mast, the shattered hull.

Today is Valentine's Day. I walk to the store
to buy a box of chocolates for my wife.
As I walk, I have no idea whose hands
made the shoes that hug my feet,
or why the produce at the super market
glows like numbers on the stock exchange.

There is sweetness in this world,
but it has a price. You are the price.

Source: "Letter to a Cockroach, Now Dead and Mixed Into a Bar of Chocolate" first appeared in *The Kenyon Review* and is reprinted with permission of the author.

14

TEXT STRUCTURE
From "Letter to a Cockroach, Now Dead and
Mixed Into a Bar of Chocolate"

**Letter to a Cockroach, Now Dead and Mixed Into a Bar of Chocolate
by Matthew Olzmann**

Regulations allow for, on average, sixty insect fragments
per hundred grams of chocolate
in America. You are pulverized.
The thorax, the head, the legs that no longer twitch.
Invisible and milk-smooth.
Nothing harbors a secret like sweetness.

real life example

truism

Centuries ago, the Sirens understood
this statute. Each sank their knowledge
inside a voice of chimes and kisses,
hiding the ocean's stone teeth
in a mouth of mist and foam.

example from classical literature

Yesterday, waves beat against a dock in Brazil.
The quick bodies of you and your buddies
quivered across the cargo of cacao beans.
You couldn't possibly comprehend: the beans
on their way to the grinder, just as those ancient sailors
couldn't envision—beyond the Sirens' music—
the broken mast, the shattered hull.

Today is Valentine's Day. I walk to the store
to buy a box of chocolates for my wife.
As I walk, I have no idea whose hands
made the shoes that hug my feet,
or why the produce at the super market
glows like numbers on the stock exchange.

There is sweetness in this world,
but it has a price. You are the price.

how this relates to me

Where they are and where I am

What I wonder

11- Minute Poem

real life example → truism → literary example → how it relates to me today → Question about the truism

Façade

Glitter sprinkled on elegantly,
roses piped on smoothly,
buttercream frosting laid down evenly,
the charms of the outer layer of cake—
elegance and art laid out on a platter.
You dig in and pause for the deliciousness,
but it doesn't come.

Like Lorraine's mother in *The Pigman*
with her beautiful face, silky
brown hair, gleaming smile.
A pleasing presence, until
she opened her mouth.
Rude and ill-mannered,
insulting and disrespectful,
judgmental yet protective.
She snuck and stole like a thief in the night.

A smile and laugh will put up my mask.
Funny, talkative, and loud
is what people think of me.
Psychologists say people who laugh too much
even at stupid things
are lonely deep inside.
I keep a façade to shadow my insecurities.
Uncertain. Stubborn. Afraid.
Imperfect.

How many people are like me?
What kind of façade do people keep?
What judgments are made of others?

Isabella Nguyen
Grade 7

To a Table

You get used a hundred times a day.
You get used by everyone. Kids, adults, teens.
You're very useful.
Without you, what would we do?

Quiet things in our life can be the most helpful.

Slaves carried your wood into the desert of Egypt
where you were made into a table,
for eating, writing and playing games
small and low to the ground
legs with ivory inlay and gold sheaths.
Preserved in a quiet sealed tomb with King Tut.

Even now I use you every day to write warmups,
    quizzes, notes.
You're important in my life.
On you, I built a roller coaster for Ms. Beltran's
    science class;
a topographical map of Mt. Fuji with birch plywood
    supplied by Ms. Sauter
Last night on you I ate pizza with my family.
I'm using you right now to write this poem.

I always wonder if you mind being used
    or written on.
Hopefully you don't
but we'll never know.
You can't talk.
There are a lot of tables.
Maybe you're special.

Moses Herrera
Grade 10

15

TEACHING NOTES
for "Parting"

WRITE.

1 Freewrite for 3 minutes (then set aside).

> think of something that happened when you were little, something that didn't make sense -- but now looking back, you wish you could change things.

*Nobody starts with a blank page.

READ.

Notice:
- the spillover stanza -- enjambment
- the italics
- the repetition (darkness)
- the "story" the poem tells is really in the middle

2 Read the poem. Aloud. Slowly. Read it again, and this time everyone should underline parts they find striking. Discuss the parts they notice. Name the craft. Notice the parts.

GET THE STRUCTURE.

3 Reveal the chunked poem. (Students copy the chunks.) Re-read the poem, watching the movement of the structure.

Making Sense of Something Painful

| what I was too young to understand | what happened long ago | what I wish for now |

WRITE.

4 Invite students to write a poem. Right now you have
- A page of thoughts
- Examples of craft you like
- A text structure

See what you come up with!
Use any of those, change any, and see what you write in the next minutes.

Parting
by Octavio Quintanilla

There was a time
I had no word for *darkness,*
and so I said, *darkness.*

I had no word to say *devotion,*
and so I said, *Two sons
grieving one mother.*

A time came when our parents
sat under a tree
and cried for us, their sons

on their way
to a new country.

When I try to return to my boyhood,

sometimes I end
with my head

on my mother's lap.

Source: "Parting" printed with permission of the author.

TEXT STRUCTURE
From "Parting"

Parting
by Octavio Quintanilla

There was a time
I had no word for *darkness,*
and so I said, *darkness.*

I had no word to say *devotion,*
and so I said, *Two sons*
grieving one mother.

What I was too young to understand

A time came when our parents
sat under a tree
and cried for us, their sons

on their way
to a new country.

What happened long ago

When I try to return to my boyhood,

sometimes I end
with my head

on my mother's lap.

What I wish for now

Making Sense of Something Painful

| *What I was too young to understand* | *What happened long ago* | *What I wish for now* |

Ocean

I would not step in the
water. I was thinking
just get it over with.

My cousin was jumping
and splashing in the water. I was covered
in sand, too scared to wash it off.

I was so hot and lonely not
in the water.
I was scared to go in.

I just wish I got in
and played with my family and washed
the sand off.

Gigi Howard
Grade 4

I Am Nino

I wonder what it would be like if my mom was here.
I hear her voice.
I see her nowhere.
I want to see her.
I am Nino.

I pretend she's here.
I feel her presence.
I touch her heart.
I worry that she will never come back.
I cry for her.
I am Nino.

I understand she's gone.
I say that she's not gone.
I dream that she will come back.
I hope that I'm going to be okay.
I am Nino.

Nino Tambunga
Grade 7

Too Young to Understand

Once I was
too young
to understand hunting.

My dad
dressed me up
in camo.

And put me in the
truck with
a gun.

He drove me
to
Grandpaws.

He took
me to a deer stand.

We climbed high.

I saw a deer with antlers.

And then bam!

The deer fell
and did not get back up.

Tucker Lundin
Grade 4

WRITE.

1 Freewrite for
3 minutes
(then set aside).

Think of something
or someone that
you could tell was
hurt in some way.

What did you see?
How did you know?

*Nobody starts with a blank page.

READ.

Notice:
- direct address
  (2nd person pov)
- Simile
- images ~ so
  clear!

2 Read the poem.
Aloud. Slowly.
Read it again, and this
time everyone should underline
parts they find striking. Discuss
the parts they notice. Name the
craft. Notice the parts.

GET THE STRUCTURE.

3 Reveal the chunked poem. (Students copy
the chunks.) Re-read the poem, watching
the movement of the structure.

Empathizing With a Wounded Creature

| who/what you are and what you are doing | what bad thing happened to you | your situation now | a question for you |

WRITE.

4 Invite students to write a poem.
Right now you have
- A page of thoughts
- Examples of craft you like
- A text structure

See what you come up with!
Use any of those, change any, and see what you write
in the next minutes.

The Falcon
by Leslie Contreras Schwartz

Peregrine falcon,
the students stare at you
fixed by a rope on a broken log.

Wing tips cut
by a propeller or bridge
as you hunted in morning light.

Now you are bound,
the glare of the school's auditorium
more blinding than the sun.

Your eye, like a blackberry,
one of your talons severed in half,
you stand reduced, impassive,

despite the tough bands of steel gray,
the sturdy earth-colored coat.

What use is flight, my friend,
when all around is no sky, no stream, no shore.

Source: "The Falcon" from *Fuego* (St. Julian Press, 2016) is reprinted with permission of the author.

The Falcon
by Leslie Contreras Schwartz

Peregrine falcon,
the students stare at you
fixed by a rope on a broken log.

what you are and what you're doing

Wing tips cut
by a propeller or bridge
as you hunted in morning light.

what (bad!) thing happened to you

Now you are bound,
the glare of the school's auditorium
more blinding than the sun.

Your eye, like a blackberry,
one of your talons severed in half,
you stand reduced, impassive,

despite the tough bands of steel gray,
the sturdy earth-colored coat.

Your situation now

What use is flight, my friend,
when all around is no sky, no stream, no shore.

a question for you

Empathizing With a Wounded Creature

who/what you are and what you are doing	what bad thing happened to you	your situation now	a question for you

The Cat

O, white cat
We look at you with sorrow
Sitting on the black concrete

Your skin cut open
By those too dark dogs
As you wandered the yard
Your icy blue eyes
Still glassy and piercing
Still staring at me

Your pearl coat
Is stained red
Patches of pink

You sit there
The sun burning your skin
But grace still lurks in your limbs

O, cat, why must you burn without sin?

Emi Ramirez
Grade 8

Painful Hide-and-Seek

Little brother
crying in the bathroom
holding your foot

pinkie toe cut
while you were looking for me
as we played hide-and-seek

bloody footprints led me
to your current location
on the closed toilet lid.

What happened
and are you okay?

Quincy Hodges
Grade 7

WRITE.

1 Freewrite for 3 minutes (then set aside).

think of a time when you wanted to do something or go somewhere — and you had to convince someone else that it was a good idea. Write about that time.

*Nobody starts with a blank page.

READ.

Notice:
• present tense narration
• 3rd person
• rich sensory details
• italicized voice dialogue

2 Read the poem. Aloud. Slowly. Read it again, and this time everyone should underline parts they find striking. Discuss the parts they notice. Name the craft. Notice the parts.

GET THE STRUCTURE.

3 Reveal the chunked poem. (Students copy the chunks.) Re-read the poem, watching the movement of the structure.

Let's Go!

| what I do while I dream of going | what the other person is doing | what I do before bringing it up | how I bring up the subject | their response |

WRITE.

4 Invite students to write a poem. Right now you have
• A page of thoughts
• Examples of craft you like
• A text structure

See what you come up with!
Use any of those, change any, and see what you write in the next minutes.

Fixing on the Next Star
by Patricia Smith

Before 1916 and 1970, more than half a million African-Americans left the South and migrated to Chicago.

Mamas go quietly crazy, dizzied by the possibilities
of a kitchen, patiently plucking hairs from the skin
of supper. Swinging children from thick forearms,
they hum stanzas riddled with Alabama hue and promises
Jesus may have made. Homes swerve on foundations
while, inside, the women wash stems and shreds of syrup
from their palms and practice contented smiles,
remembering that it's a sin to damn this ritual or foul
the heat-sparkled air with any language less than prayer.

And they wait for their loves, men of marbled shoulders
and exploded nails, their faces grizzled landscapes
of scar and descent. These men stain every room
they enter, drag with them a stench of souring iron.
The dulled wives narrow their eyes, busy themselves
with clanging and stir, then feed the sweating
soldiers whole feasts built upon okra and the peppered
necks of chickens. After the steam dies, chewing
is all there is—the slurp of spiced oil, the crunch
of bone, suck of marrow. And then the conversation,
which never changes, even over the children's squeals:
They say it's better up there, it begins, and it is always
the woman who says this, and the man lowers his head
to the table and feels the day collapse beneath his shirt.

**Fixing on the Next Star
by Patricia Smith**

*Between 1916 and 1970, more than half a million African-Americans left the South
and migrated to Chicago.*

Mamas go quietly crazy, dizzied by the possibilities
of a kitchen, patiently plucking hairs from the skin
of supper. Swinging children from thick forearms,
they hum stanzas riddled with Alabama hue and promises
Jesus may have made. Homes swerve on foundations
while, inside, the women wash stems and shreds of syrup
from their palms and practice contented smiles,
remembering that it's a sin to damn this ritual or foul
the heat-sparkled air with any language less than prayer.

What they do while they dream of going

And they wait for their loves, men of marbled shoulders
and exploded nails, their faces grizzled landscapes
of scar and descent. These men stain every room
they enter, drag with them a stench of souring iron.

What the other persons (men) are doing

The dulled wives narrow their eyes, busy themselves
with clanging and stir, then feed the sweating
soldiers whole feasts built upon okra and the peppered
necks of chickens. After the steam dies, chewing
is all there is—the slurp of spiced oil, the crunch
of bone, suck of marrow. And then the conversation,
which never changes, even over the children's squeals:
They say it's better up there, it begins, and it is always
the woman who says this, and the man lowers his head
to the table and feels the day collapse beneath his shirt.

What the women do before bringing it up

how they bring up the subject

their response

Let's Go!

| what I do while I dream of going | what the other person is doing | what I do before bringing it up | how I bring up the subject | their response |

Wishing on La Perla

There was a time I wanted to go
to a Mexican restaurant that I liked.

But my family wanted to go
someplace new.

When we went, I opened the door
and the place smelled like feet and vinegar.
There was an octopus sandwich,
and shrimp that seemed like it had been lying
on the ocean floor forever, smelling
like expired milk.

The food tasted like re-heated McDonald's.

I told my family that we should
have gone to the restaurant that I
    wanted to go to
in the first place.

They didn't listen, but later said:
"You were right. Next time we'll
    listen to you."

Benjamin Z. Ruiz
Grade 8

Outside

I was trying to convince my uncle
on this sunny, breezy day
to take me outside to play basketball.

He was lying on the couch
watching The Office. He always
watches that stupid show.

I wondered how I should approach him.
Should I just tell him, or do him a favor first?

Sweat coming down my face, I asked.
He said, "Yeah, go get your shoes."

I burst with joy, jumping in the air.
My day was the best.

Joseph Gomez II
Grade 9

WRITE.

1 Freewrite for 3 minutes (then set aside).

> think about things that are happening in the world, things you have learned in the last few months.
>
> Make a quick list of facts.

*Nobody starts with a blank page.

READ.

> Notice:
> • list poem
> • Specificity
> • Metaphor (baskets)
> • Enjambment

2 Read the poem. Aloud. Slowly.
Read it again, and this time everyone should underline parts they find striking. Discuss the parts they notice. Name the craft. Notice the parts.

GET THE STRUCTURE.

3 Reveal the chunked poem. (Students copy the chunks.) Re-read the poem, watching the movement of the structure.

> What I Learned About the World
>
> | What new thing I learned about the world (x3) | a new thing I learned about someone close to me | how it made me feel | one more new thing I learned about the world |

WRITE.

4 Invite students to write a poem.
Right now you have
- A page of thoughts
- Examples of craft you like
- A text structure

See what you come up with!
Use any of those, change any, and see what you write in the next minutes.

What I Learned This Week
by Angela Narciso Torres

There are no more fireflies in Northern Indiana.
Marine life in Lake Erie is dying out because

fish are ingesting plastic microbeads used in
cosmetics to defoliate dead skin. Yellow X's mark

seven trees on our street that workers will axe
next week. Ash borers have eaten them alive

so they cannot absorb water or light. This week I learned
that my mother is losing dexterity in both hands.

But when I play Bach's Ave Maria on the piano, she lifts
her head, motions me to move her wheelchair closer.

She leans over the keyboard to try the melody, finding
the right notes each time. Her fingers can barely strike

the keys, but I hear them. Some say music memory
is the last to go. Still, I have no windfalls

for the empty baskets of my mother's eyes.
When I returned from Manila, the peonies I'd left

in half-blossom were thwarted by summer storms.
A bud that will not bloom is called a bullet.

Source: "What I Learned This Week" first appeared in *Spoon River Poetry Review* and is reprinted with permission of the author.

What I Learned This Week
by Angela Narciso Torres

There are no more fireflies in Northern Indiana.
Marine life in Lake Erie is dying out because

fish are ingesting plastic microbeads used in
cosmetics to defoliate dead skin. Yellow X's mark

new things I learned about the world

seven trees on our street that workers will axe
next week. Ash borers have eaten them alive

so they cannot absorb water or light. This week I learned
that my mother is losing dexterity in both hands.

But when I play Bach's Ave Maria on the piano, she lifts
her head, motions me to move her wheelchair closer.

She leans over the keyboard to try the melody, finding
the right notes each time. Her fingers can barely strike

the keys, but I hear them. Some say music memory
is the last to go. Still, I have no windfalls

something I learned about my mother

for the empty baskets of my mother's eyes.
When I returned from Manila, the peonies I'd left

in half-blossom were thwarted by summer storms.
A bud that will not bloom is called a bullet.

how it made me feel

one more new thing I learned about the world

What I Learned About the World

What new thing I learned about the world (x3)	a new thing I learned about someone close to me	how it made me feel	one more new thing I learned about the world

Horizon

I learned there's a lot of traffic downtown. When it's humid
there's dark cloud, and when you go outside
mosquitos attack you. I learned that marine life is slowly
dying, and straws get stuck in turtles' throats.
This week I learned that my Tia would always be there
for me. She helped make my quinceñera invitations,
the save the dates, photos and decorations.
Even when my mom doesn't know how to tie my corset,
my Tia is there to help lace up the back of my dress.
When she puts her nerdy glasses on, my Tia is focused,
and I'm so grateful. She helps me a lot. I also learned
to notice the sunset, how the sun at the horizon
looks cut in half, and the sky looks like cotton candy,
streaked orange, red, pink, even purple, yellow and blue.
When the sun goes down, it's like my energy,
like my mindset when things feel easy and I'm calm.

Nayelie Muñoz
Grade 8

WRITE.

1 Freewrite for 3 minutes (then set aside).

What do you know about the etymology (origin) of your name? What do you wish it meant? What would you like the history and meaning of your name to be?

*Nobody starts with a blank page.

READ.

Notice:
- extended list (aka pitchfork aka enumeratio)

2 Read the poem. Aloud. Slowly.
Read it again, and this time everyone should underline parts they find striking. Discuss the parts they notice. Name the craft. Notice the parts.

GET THE STRUCTURE.

3 Reveal the chunked poem. (Students copy the chunks.) Re-read the poem, watching the movement of the structure.

Etymology of My Name

| What my name means | a memory | where all you can find it | another way I like to interpret my name |

WRITE.

4 Invite students to write a poem.
Right now you have
- A page of thoughts
- Examples of craft you like
- A text structure

See what you come up with!
Use any of those, change any, and see what you write in the next minutes.

Maria
by Natalia Treviño

Maria: plural of mare,
Latin for seas.

Mar, me mareas.
The ocean seas.

Dark spots on the moon,
were once thought lunar oceans.

As a girl, marinera, marinera,
I floated en el mar every day, on a hot, rubbery inner tube,

my mother next to me, in her tube,
holding my hand as the sea stung our sunburnt eyes,

healed our mosquito-bitten backs
lifted us over her white lips and cliffs.

If we let go of each other on time,
trusted we would not be swallowed,

she rushed us, our tumbling bodies
powerless to shore.

This sea, seawater, maria on Earth,
liquid solution, the saline in our blood,

in our nostrils, in our eyes, a living water,
a hearing water, scientists say,

who fills Earth's deepest wombs and wounds
who holds us for a time, floats us in her

dark body of bodies, seals us in thick muscle
when we can breathe her pure liquid in

before it rises to a lip
        before it rushes

                our tumbling bodies
                    powerless to shore.

If Maria's name is an accident
of etymology,

I am only more mariada.

Babies point to the moon,
say *ma.*

Source: "Maria" from the chapbook *VirginX* (Finishing Line Press, 2019) is reprinted with permission of the author.

Maria
by Natalia Treviño

Maria: plural of mare,
Latin for seas.

Mar, me mareas.
The ocean seas.

Dark spots on the moon,
were once thought lunar oceans.

What my name means

As a girl, marinera, marinera,
I floated en el mar every day, on a hot, rubbery inner tube,

my mother next to me, in her tube,
holding my hand as the sea stung our sunburnt eyes,

healed our mosquito-bitten backs
lifted us over her white lips and cliffs.

If we let go of each other on time,
trusted we would not be swallowed,

she rushed us, our tumbling bodies
powerless to shore.

a memory

This sea, seawater, maria on Earth,
liquid solution, the saline in our blood,

in our nostrils, in our eyes, a living water,
a hearing water, scientists say,

who fills Earth's deepest wombs and wounds
who holds us for a time, floats us in her

dark body of bodies, seals us in thick muscle
when we can breathe her pure liquid in

before it rises to a lip
        before it rushes

            our tumbling bodies
                powerless to shore.

where all you can find it

If Maria's name is an accident
of etymology,

I am only more mariada.

Babies point to the moon,
say *ma*.

another way I like to interpret my name

Etymology of My Name

| What my name means | a memory | Where all you can find it | another way I like to interpret my name |

My Name

Clarissa is my name,
said like kla-riss-ah
Latin for clarus

Clear
Brilliant
Famous

When I was a little girl
people would ask me what my name is
and I would respond, saying "sissa"
Now my nickname will
forever be
sissa

I especially love my name
when I'm in Mexico, because
my name sounds so sexy
It sounds like fireworks
sparking then going into the
sky and popping

It has a harsh "E"
kla-ee-sah.
I feel so powerful when I say
my name in
Spanish.

Clarissa Gutierrez
Grade 9

READ.

Notice:
- Claim is in the 1st 4 words, evidence stacked afterwards in concrete images
- personification (heron beckons)
- metaphor

WRITE.

1 Freewrite for 3 minutes (then set aside).

If you had something serious on your mind, where is someplace outdoors where you would think it out?

Write about that.

*Nobody starts with a blank page.

2 Read the poem. Aloud. Slowly.
Read it again, and this time everyone should underline parts they find striking. Discuss the parts they notice. Name the craft. Notice the parts.

GET THE STRUCTURE.

3 Reveal the chunked poem. (Students copy the chunks.) Re-read the poem, watching the movement of the structure.

A Place to Think It Out

| my mood | what I see in the distance | what I see nearby | how something changes my thinking |

WRITE.

4 Invite students to write a poem.
Right now you have
- A page of thoughts
- Examples of craft you like
- A text structure

See what you come up with!
Use any of those, change any, and see what you write in the next minutes.

On the Shoreline
by Laura Van Prooyen

Her vision is unreliable, as are her prayers.

She begs the lake to guide her, but expects nothing

more than this mantra of lapping. A boat

trolls by, the fishermen nearly indistinguishable

from trees. In this light, the great blue heron

on the dock could be anything: a child, or lovers

folding themselves into each other. It opens its wings;

the span is alarming. He beckons, urges her

to walk upon the water. She offers her foot to the surface,

and for a moment, she believes it is possible.

On the Shoreline
by Laura Van Prooyen

Her vision is unreliable, as are her prayers.

She begs the lake to guide her, but expects nothing

more than this mantra of lapping. A boat

trolls by, the fishermen nearly indistinguishable

from trees. In this light, the great blue heron

on the dock could be anything: a child, or lovers

folding themselves into each other. It opens its wings;

the span is alarming. It beckons, urges her

to walk upon the water. She offers her foot to the surface,

and for a moment, she believes it is possible.

my mood

what I see in the distance

what I see nearby

how some-thing changes my thinking

A Place to Think It Out

| my mood | what I see in the distance | what I see nearby | how something changes my thinking |

Third Floor View

His motivation was as unclear as his purpose.
He begs to fade away as the buildings do
on the rainy day. Limestone and glass facades
disappear in the haze. Only the tips
of low-rise church steeples find their way
into his third-floor gaze. Below he sees the lives
of the city. Umbrellas dance across the streets
seeking shelter from the deluge. Neon signs
illuminate a soft glow in the torrent. He
takes a deep breath and with a refreshed
mind, finds his place.

Julen Navarette
Grade 10

READ.

WRITE.

1 Freewrite for 3 minutes (then set aside).

Think about an older relative who asks you to do something (get a jar from the fridge, rub their shoulders, etc.) Write about that.

*Nobody starts with a blank page.

Notice:
• metaphor
• images
• sensory details
• Sounds
• enjambment

2 Read the poem. Aloud. Slowly. Read it again, and this time everyone should underline parts they find striking. Discuss the parts they notice. Name the craft. Notice the parts.

GET THE STRUCTURE.

3 Reveal the chunked poem. (Students copy the chunks.) Re-read the poem, watching the movement of the structure.

Tender Memory

| description of the place | aside by the speaker | description of the action | how the person used to be different | what I wonder about the person | a memory of something the person would always do |

WRITE.

4 Invite students to write a poem.
Right now you have
• A page of thoughts
• Examples of craft you like
• A text structure

See what you come up with!
Use any of those, change any, and see what you write in the next minutes.

As Always, Thirty Years Between Us
by Laura Van Prooyen

My father wants me to cut his hair
in the laundry room, where the rotary phone
still hangs on the wall. Here, I took
and made so many calls to boys
he disapproved of. This is an old story.
A father, daughter, half-regrets. I fold over
his ear the way he tells me to and trim.
Nothing's left of the lush, black swoop
or sideburns he always wore. I buzz
the white crown and snip stray hairs
from the bald part of his head. He's
nothing like the man whose empty
cans I used to find in the trunk
of the car. I wonder, now, how
many times he knew my secrets,
but didn't say a word. No one
really can tell you how not to mess up
your life. When I was young,
I loved the winter nights, watching
my father grease fishing reels
at the kitchen table, cranking handles,
clicking spools shut. Summer was miles
away, but he took such pleasure
getting ready. Especially when it came
to sharpening his fillet knife. I leaned
my shoulder close to his, shut my eyes
to better hear him whisk
that blade across a wet, black stone.

Source: "As Always, Thirty Years Between Us" from *Our House Was on Fire* (Ashland Poetry Press, 2015) is reprinted with permission of the author.

As Always, Thirty Years Between Us
by Laura Van Prooyen

My father wants me to cut his hair
in the laundry room, where the rotary phone
still hangs on the wall. Here, I took
and made so many calls to boys
he disapproved of. This is an old story.
A father, daughter, half-regrets. I fold over
his ear the way he tells me to and trim.
Nothing's left of the lush, black swoop
or sideburns he always wore. I buzz
the white crown and snip stray hairs
from the bald part of his head. He's
nothing like the man whose empty
cans I used to find in the trunk
of the car. I wonder, now, how
many times he knew my secrets,
but didn't say a word. No one
really can tell you how not to mess up
your life. When I was young,
I loved the winter nights, watching
my father grease fishing reels
at the kitchen table, cranking handles,
clicking spools shut. Summer was miles
away, but he took such pleasure
getting ready. Especially when it came
to sharpening his fillet knife. I leaned
my shoulder close to his, shut my eyes
to better hear him whisk
that blade across a wet, black stone.

description of the place

aside

description of the action

how he used to be different

what I wonder

a memory of something

Tender Memory

description of the place	aside by the speaker	description of the action	how the person used to be different	what I wonder about the person	a memory of something the person would always do

As Always, Aunt Amy

My aunt asks me to grab the piping bag from the
cabinet in the front room, where the whole family loses
to my seven-year-old cousin in card games. Here,
we always gather around the tiny Christmas tree propped up on
the side table. This is a story of family traditions. An aunt
who makes an effort to keep them going. I scoop some
icing into the bag, snip the end, and begin piping.
It seeps out smoothly, making the gingerbread
look more alive with each squeeze of the bag.
My aunt ices a smile, two dots for eyes, and a little curl of hair.
She hate changes. She's had the same job for 30 years
and will never leave her hometown. I wonder
if my aunt always thought this way, and if she
will ever change her thinking. When I was young,
I loved the summertime when the whole family
would reunite at a house on the lake,
rolling down the grassy hill with my cousins, trapping
lightning bugs between our tiny palms. My aunt
would sit on the back porch, a Diet Coke in hand,
watching us run around with a smile on her face.

Sadie Clyne
College Student

WRITE.

1 Freewrite for 3 minutes (then set aside).

Imagine you could write a postcard to someone who's not around you right now.
What do you wish you could say?

*Nobody starts with a blank page.

READ.

Notice:
- metaphors
- list/ pitchforks
- personification
- feeling named by what you'd say to someone
- Enjambment

2 Read the poem. Aloud. Slowly.
Read it again, and this time everyone should underline parts they find striking. Discuss the parts they notice. Name the craft. Notice the parts.

GET THE STRUCTURE.

3 Reveal the chunked poem. (Students copy the chunks.) Re-read the poem, watching the movement of the structure.

This Strong Feeling (in Metaphor)

| this feeling means (something I smell) | this feeling also means (something I see) | this feeling means (opposite things) | Images to show how big this feeling is |

WRITE.

4 Invite students to write a poem.
Right now you have
- A page of thoughts
- Examples of craft you like
- A text structure

See what you come up with!
Use any of those, change any, and see what you write in the next minutes.

Postcard From Texas
by Laura Van Prooyen

This morning, miss you means the hawthorn's

blooming, air so sweet it threatens to attract bees.

Miss you is a street full of pecans that roll under

my feet. I falter, yes, but I do not fall. Miss you

means falling, means I'm still standing, means

this distance feels bigger than Texas, than long tall

clouds high enough to be laced with snow.

Source: "Postcard From Texas" first appeared in *Poet Lore* and is reprinted with permission of the author.

Postcard From Texas
by Laura Van Prooyen

This morning, miss you means the hawthorn's

blooming, air so sweet it threatens to attract bees.

Miss you is a street full of pecans that roll under

my feet. I falter, yes, but I do not fall. Miss you

means falling, means I'm still standing, means

this distance feels bigger than Texas, than long tall

clouds high enough to be laced with snow.

This feeling means
— Something
I smell

It means
Something I see

It means
— opposite
things

images to show
— how
big this
feeling is

This Strong Feeling (in Metaphor)

this feeling means (Something I smell)	this feeling also means (Something I see)	this feeling means (opposite things)	Images to show how big this feeling is

Postcard to Papi

I miss your smell, which attracts
   butterflies
to my heart. I wish you were near,
   so you could see
the flowers bloom over my feet.
I want you here, but I don't know
   where you are.
I miss you like the miles between
   Texas and Mexico.

Azucena Sanchez-Vega
Grade 4

Can't Wait

Can't wait means the turkey
   roasted, that brings
everyone to the dinner table. Can't wait
   is a city full
of windows that shine, that never stop
   shining. Can't wait
means afraid of the future, but never
   could be more
excited. It means not even a million
   years could stop
me from having this feeling.

Lennon Horsley
Grade 7

To My Pup

The love I try to send to you
smells of that one beach you loved.
I may not see you, but I sense you
walking with me on your way
down the rainbow road. I can feel
your soft head there when I need comfort.
I fall, but your paws lift me back up,
as if I were already standing. You
may not be here, but because of my choice,
you won't be in any more pain. Enjoy dancing
with your haloed friend and have fun
   in the clouds.

Lily-Ann Ackerman
Grade 4

WRITE.

1 Freewrite for
3 minutes
(then set aside).

Think of some of your first memories from when you were little.

Describe as much as you can.

*Nobody starts with a blank page.

READ.

Notice:
• repetition of beginning of sentence
• how the specific images work on a reader
• use of 2nd person

2 Read the poem.
Aloud. Slowly.
Read it again, and this time everyone should underline parts they find striking. Discuss the parts they notice. Name the craft. Notice the parts.

GET THE STRUCTURE.

3 Reveal the chunked poem. (Students copy the chunks.) Re-read the poem, watching the movement of the structure.

What You Can and Cannot Have (List)

| You can't have... | but you can have/do/know | you can learn... | what you throw away | what you keep |

WRITE.

4 Invite students to write a poem.
Right now you have
• A page of thoughts
• Examples of craft you like
• A text structure

See what you come up with!
Use any of those, change any, and see what you write in the next minutes.

One of Those Days
by Laura Van Prooyen

—after Barbara Ras

You can't have it all, but you can have old asbestos shingles
painted a brand new blue. You can have
the crooked-jaw black cat that sleeps on your legs,
follows you to the kitchen, curls beside you on your chair.
You can have the hand of a 10-year-old on your knee,
lifting one finger at a time for you to paint silver
on each little nail. You can travel to a new city,
alert and alive as you walk on unknown streets, you can
sit beside the sparkling ocean, but you can't change
sorrow. You can have love, even when it's like apple cider
vinegar, that sour cure for so many ills. You can take
your father out for a fresh peach sundae, his dentures clacking
a lifetime of loss and he can tell you the exact etch and cut
he wants on his own grave stone. You can have cattails
in the ditch, the long bus ride where you were the first one on
and the last one off, and you knew every child at every stop.
You can move closer to joy, your yard flowering
with *bougainvillea* and *esperanza* and still regret touching
hairless baby gerbils the morning the mother
killed and buried in wood shavings her whole brood.
You can have manure in spring and call it sweet. You can't
count on faith to stroke your cheek, but your mother
hauls a pair of roller skates down from the attic, the ancient ones
with a key, you can unlock them and slide them to your size.
In a pile of junk, you can still find boots that fit. And when you sort
through childhoods stiff with mold, you learn about acceptance
as you quietly throw clothes into garbage bags, drive them
to a dumpster, give up what will never be missed. You
won't know in what ways you failed, hundreds of possibilities
thread your sheets. You can't have it all, but you can
still count on the evergreen. You can summon the sound
of your dad's electric clippers, of your mother's metal rake.
Your fingers scrape over pebbled ground like tines.
You gather cuttings, the sun warm on your back.

Source: "One of Those Days" first appeared in *Spoon River Poetry Review* and is reprinted with permission of the author.

One of Those Days
by Laura Van Prooyen

—after Barbara Ras

You can't have it all, but you can have old asbestos shingles
painted a brand new blue. You can have
the crooked-jaw black cat that sleeps on your legs,
follows you to the kitchen, curls beside you on your chair.
You can have the hand of a 10-year-old on your knee,
lifting one finger at a time for you to paint silver
on each little nail. You can travel to a new city,
alert and alive as you walk on unknown streets, you can
sit beside the sparkling ocean, but you can't change
sorrow. You can have love, even when it's like apple cider
vinegar, that sour cure for so many ills. You can take
your father out for a fresh peach sundae, his dentures clacking
a lifetime of loss and he can tell you the exact etch and cut
he wants on his own grave stone. You can have cattails
in the ditch, the long bus ride where you were the first one on
and the last one off, and you knew every child at every stop.

You can move closer to joy, your yard flowering
with *bougainvillea* and *esperanza* and still regret touching
hairless baby gerbils the morning the mother
killed and buried in wood shavings her whole brood.
You can have manure in spring and call it sweet. You can't
count on faith to stroke your cheek, but your mother
hauls a pair of roller skates down from the attic, the ancient ones
with a key, you can unlock them and slide them to your size.
In a pile of junk, you can still find boots that fit. And when you sort
through childhoods stiff with mold, you learn about acceptance
as you quietly throw clothes into garbage bags, drive them
to a dumpster, give up what will never be missed. You
won't know in what ways you failed, hundreds of possibilities
thread your sheets. You can't have it all, but you can
still count on the evergreen. You can summon the sound
of your dad's electric clippers, of your mother's metal rake.
Your fingers scrape over pebbled ground like tines.
You gather cuttings, the sun warm on your back.

Handwritten annotations:
- you can't have
- but you can have/ Know/ do...
- you can learn
- What you throw away
- what you Keep

What You Can and Cannot Have (List)

| you can't have... | but you can have/ do/ Know | you can learn... | what you throw away | what you Keep |

What You Can and Cannot Have

You can't have it all, but you can have
blood wrenching mosquito bites scarring your skin.
You can have scorching Texas summer days
and Seattle rainy nights. You can have 1,000-piece puzzles
perfectly put together by your scraggly-haired little brother.
You can have overly tan skin from sitting too long by the edge
of the water in refreshing salty air. You can hold
the hand of grandma as you finish scarfing down *arroz y frijoles*.
You can learn to keep your hands far away from the oven
and that chicken always needs more time. You can know
that mother knows best, even when she doesn't
and that to respect your elders is the most important
thing in life. You can throw out any sign of tears and scars
from the torture of fifth grade and middle school.
No more teasing. Imperfections may still be there,
but they don't matter anymore. You know that the love
of those who know you, truly is all you'll ever need.

Sarah R. Guerrero
Grade 10

TEACHING NOTES
for "She Inherits His Steady Hand"

WRITE.

1 Freewrite for 3 minutes (then set aside).

Think of someone who needed help because they weren't able to do something.

Write about that.

*Nobody starts with a blank page.

READ.

Notice:
- It's one sentence!
- Simile
- Lyric moment

Where [this was happening / this was happening / this was happening]

2 Read the poem. Aloud. Slowly. Read it again, and this time everyone should underline parts they find striking. Discuss the parts they notice. Name the craft. Notice the parts.

GET THE STRUCTURE.

3 Reveal the chunked poem. (Students copy the chunks.) Re-read the poem, watching the movement of the structure.

Lyric Moment

| When this was | Who needed help | 3 things that were happening at the same time |

WRITE.

4 Invite students to write a poem.
Right now you have
- A page of thoughts
- Examples of craft you like
- A text structure

See what you come up with!
Use any of those, change any, and see what you write in the next minutes.

She Inherits His Steady Hand
by Laura Van Prooyen

The year of his decline, the diminishing
Marine sat by the aviary where finches
flung seeds, where his five-year-old

granddaughter lifted the spoon, where
he mimicked her gesture,
opening his mouth to be fed like a bird.

Source: "She Inherits His Steady Hand" first appeared in *Poet Lore* and is reprinted with permission of the author.

She Inherits His Steady Hand
by Laura Van Prooyen

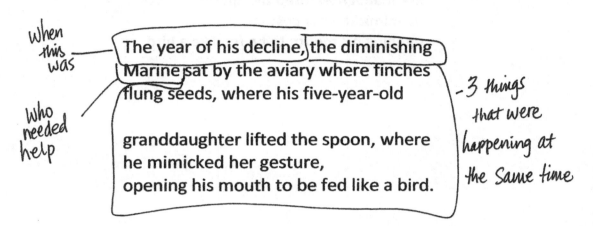

When this was

Who needed help

The year of his decline, the diminishing
Marine sat by the aviary where finches
flung seeds, where his five-year-old

granddaughter lifted the spoon, where
he mimicked her gesture,
opening his mouth to be fed like a bird.

—3 things that were happening at the same time

Lyric Moment

When this was

Who needed help

3 things that were happening at the same time

The Help

The year of his sorrow,
the lonely student
was sitting in a deep dark place
full of sadness, evil and unhappiness,
when his 14-year-old brother
stood up and yelled, *Snap out of it!*
and took him outside to play basketball,
throwing water on his face.
The lonely boy found some joy.

Joseph Gomez II
Grade 9

Classic Poems

WRITE.

1 Freewrite for 3 minutes (then set aside).

Think of something you made, Something which you were proud of at the time.

Write about it.

*Nobody starts with a blank page.

READ.

Notice :
- apostrophe (direct address)
- rhyming couplets
- iambic pentameter
- personification

2 Read the poem. Aloud. Slowly.
Read it again, and this time everyone should underline parts they find striking. Discuss the parts they notice. Name the craft. Notice the parts.

GET THE STRUCTURE.

3 Reveal the chunked poem. (Students copy the chunks.) Re-read the poem, watching the movement of the structure.

What I Would Say to the Thing I Made

| What you are | What happened when other people saw you | What I did next | What you should stay away from | what to say when people ask about your family |

WRITE.

4 Invite students to write a poem.
Right now you have
- A page of thoughts
- Examples of craft you like
- A text structure

See what you come up with!
Use any of those, change any, and see what you write in the next minutes.

The Author to Her Book
by Anne Bradstreet

Thou ill-form'd offspring of my feeble brain,
Who after birth didst by my side remain,
Till snatched from thence by friends, less wise than true,
Who thee abroad, expos'd to publick view,
Made thee in raggs, halting to th' press to trudge,
Where errors were not lessened (all may judg).
At thy return my blushing was not small,
My rambling brat (in print) should mother call,
I cast thee by as one unfit for light,
Thy Visage was so irksome in my sight;
Yet being mine own, at length affection would
Thy blemishes amend, if so I could:
I wash'd thy face, but more defects I saw,
And rubbing off a spot, still made a flaw.
I stretched thy joynts to make thee even feet,
Yet still thou run'st more hobling then is meet;
In better dress to trim thee was my mind,
But nought save home-spun Cloth, i' th' house I find.
In this array 'mongst Vulgars mayst thou roam.
In Criticks hands, beware thou dost not come;
And take thy way where yet thou art not known,
If for thy Father askt, say, thou hadst none:
And for thy Mother, she alas is poor,
Which caus'd her thus to send thee out of door.

Source: Anne Bradstreet, "The Author to Her Book," *The Tenth Muse,* 1650.

The Author to Her Book
by Anne Bradstreet

Thou ill-form'd offspring of my feeble brain, *what you are*
Who after birth didst by my side remain,

Till snatched from thence by friends, less wise than true, *what happened when other people saw you*
Who thee abroad, expos'd to publick view,
Made thee in raggs, halting to th' press to trudge,
Where errors were not lessened (all may judg).
At thy return my blushing was not small,
My rambling brat (in print) should mother call,

I cast thee by as one unfit for light, *what I did next*
Thy Visage was so irksome in my sight;
Yet being mine own, at length affection would
Thy blemishes amend, if so I could:
I wash'd thy face, but more defects I saw,
And rubbing off a spot, still made a flaw.
I stretched thy joynts to make thee even feet,
Yet still thou run'st more hobling then is meet;
In better dress to trim thee was my mind,
But nought save home-spun Cloth, i' th' house I find.

In this array 'mongst Vulgars mayst thou roam. *what you should stay away from*
In Criticks hands, beware thou dost not come;
And take thy way where yet thou art not known,

If for thy Father askt, say, thou hadst none: *what to say when people ask you about your family*
And for thy Mother, she alas is poor,
Which caus'd her thus to send thee out of door.

What I Would Say to the Thing I Made

What you are	What happened when other people saw you	What I did next	What you should stay away from	What to say when people ask about your family

To GyroBoy

You're a robot, a code-reader, mostly white and silver
on wheels of solid gold, created by Javan and me.
We knew what we were doing.

Your gyro-sensor measures your angle when you lean
and then combats the lean.

Gabriel said "Wow" at your self-balances.
Aidan gaped in surprise.

Our team will work out your kinks.
Next we will do battle.

Don't go near the edge of the table. If you do,
turn in a 45° angle and move away from the edge.
Keep your balance, and try to outlast the enemy.

Your parents are a program and batteries.
Your brothers are your gears and axles.
Your sisters are your supports, Lego beams.
It's a strong family.

Henry L. Schell
Grade 6

A Letter to Robo-Ball

Robo-ball, that's your name, my basketball
robot game. Students launch your catapult arm
so that they can win the candy you throw.

You were supposed to bring surprise and delight
and you did. They thought of you
as a birthday present that they can play with.

So I let them play, but don't worry
I have more Starbursts so you don't get sad
when you give them away.

Stay away from toddlers who might break you
into pieces or bullies who just want to steal
your candy heart.

If people ask, tell them your creator
had a tough time building you
out of a vending machine and a ping pong game.
Tell them your creator used his knowledge.
He knew what he was doing, and you can be proud.

Ricardo Ramos
Grade 6

26

TEACHING NOTES
for "Sonnet 43: How Do I Love Thee? Let Me Count the Ways"

WRITE.

1

Freewrite for
3 minutes
(then set aside).

> Name some of your favorite things.
> (for about 30 seconds)
>
> Choose one and make a list of what you like about it.

*Nobody starts with a blank page.

READ.

> Notice:
> 3 quatrains
> + 1 couplet
> a Petrarchan Sonnet
> ° Slant rhyme (faith/break)
> • thee = you

2

Read the poem.
Aloud. Slowly.
Read it again, and this time everyone should underline parts they find striking. Discuss the parts they notice. Name the craft. Notice the parts.

GET THE STRUCTURE.

3

Reveal the chunked poem. (Students copy the chunks.) Re-read the poem, watching the movement of the structure.

> Question and Multiple Answers
>
> | Question | one possible answer | another possible answer | another possible answer | ...and so on |

WRITE.

4

Invite students to write a poem.
Right now you have
- A page of thoughts
- Examples of craft you like
- A text structure

See what you come up with!
Use any of those, change any, and see what you write in the next minutes.

Sonnet 43:
How Do I Love Thee? Let Me Count the Ways
by Elizabeth Barrett Browning

How do I love thee? Let me count the ways.

I love thee to the depth and breadth and height

My soul can reach, when feeling out of sight

For the ends of being and ideal grace.

I love thee to the level of every day's

Most quiet need, by sun and candle-light.

I love thee freely, as men strive for right;

I love thee purely, as they turn from praise.

I love thee with the passion put to use

In my old griefs, and with my childhood's faith.

I love thee with a love I seemed to lose

With my lost saints. I love thee with the breath,

Smiles, tears, of all my life; and, if God choose,

I shall but love thee better after death.

Source: Elizabeth Barrett Browning, "Sonnet 43: How Do I Love Thee? Let Me Count the Ways," *Poems*, 1844.

TEXT STRUCTURE
From "Sonnet 43: How Do I Love Thee? Let Me Count the Ways"

26

Sonnet 43:
How Do I Love Thee? Let Me Count the Ways
by Elizabeth Barrett Browning

How do I love thee? Let me count the ways. — Question

I love thee to the depth and breadth and height
My soul can reach, when feeling out of sight
For the ends of being and ideal grace. — one possible answer

I love thee to the level of every day's
Most quiet need, by sun and candle-light. — another possible answer

I love thee freely, as men strive for right; — another

I love thee purely, as they turn from praise. — another

I love thee with the passion put to use
In my old griefs, and with my childhood's faith. — another

I love thee with a love I seemed to lose — another

With my lost saints. I love thee with the breath, — another

Smiles, tears, of all my life; and, if God choose,

I shall but love thee better after death. — another

Question and Multiple Answers

| Question | one possible answer | another possible answer | another possible answer | ...and so on |

STUDENT POEM
From "Sonnet 43: How Do I Love Thee? Let Me Count the Ways"

Pens

Why do I love Micron pens so much? Let me see.
I love approaching the display case full of different thicknesses
and colors, reaching out to grab one from the organized
slots. Thin, thick, brush-tip, felt-tip, red, black, orange, blue.
I love how easy they are to handle and control when they
touch the paper. I love the scratchy noise they make when
creating long dashes and I love the soft drawl made when shading.
I love the versatility, and how they can be used to take notes
in lectures or can be shoved in a book to save the page.
I love creating art that makes other people smile,
all with the use of a single pen.

Sadie Klein
Grade 12

WRITE.

1

Freewrite for
3 minutes
(then set aside).

(Prep: bring in pictures with interesting people. Let students choose one.)
Choose a picture with someone interesting in it. Look at the picture and jot down some things you observe about them.

*Nobody starts with a blank page.

READ.

Notice:
- Poetic form
  DRAMATIC
  MONOLOGUE

- iambic pentameter
- rhyming couplets
- narrators personality
- interruptions to his speech (and what caused them?)

2

Read the poem.
Aloud. Slowly.
Read it again, and this time everyone should underline parts they find striking. Discuss the parts they notice. Name the craft. Notice the parts.

GET THE STRUCTURE.

3

Reveal the chunked poem. (Students copy the chunks.) Re-read the poem, watching the movement of the structure.

A Picture that Tells A Story

| Who is in the picture | What people want to Know (when they look) | the answer to that question | Something unique about the person (and what happened to them) | What I want to Show you next |

WRITE.

4

Invite students to write a poem.
Right now you have
- A page of thoughts
- Examples of craft you like
- A text structure

See what you come up with!
Use any of those, change any, and see what you write in the next minutes.

My Last Duchess
by Robert Browning

FERRARA

That's my last Duchess painted on the wall,
Looking as if she were alive. I call
That piece a wonder, now; Fra Pandolf's hands
Worked busily a day, and there she stands.
Will't please you sit and look at her? I said
"Fra Pandolf" by design, for never read
Strangers like you that pictured countenance,
The depth and passion of its earnest glance,
But to myself they turned (since none puts by
The curtain I have drawn for you, but I)
And seemed as they would ask me, if they durst,
How such a glance came there; so, not the first
Are you to turn and ask thus. Sir, 'twas not
Her husband's presence only, called that spot
Of joy into the Duchess' cheek; perhaps
Fra Pandolf chanced to say, "Her mantle laps
Over my lady's wrist too much," or "Paint
Must never hope to reproduce the faint
Half-flush that dies along her throat." Such stuff
Was courtesy, she thought, and cause enough
For calling up that spot of joy. She had
A heart—how shall I say?— too soon made glad,
Too easily impressed; she liked whate'er
She looked on, and her looks went everywhere.
Sir, 'twas all one! My favour at her breast,
The dropping of the daylight in the West,
The bough of cherries some officious fool
Broke in the orchard for her, the white mule
She rode with round the terrace—all and each

(Continued)

(Continued)

Would draw from her alike the approving speech,
Or blush, at least. She thanked men—good! but thanked
Somehow—I know not how—as if she ranked
My gift of a nine-hundred-years-old name
With anybody's gift. Who'd stoop to blame
This sort of trifling? Even had you skill
In speech—which I have not—to make your will
Quite clear to such an one, and say, "Just this
Or that in you disgusts me; here you miss,
Or there exceed the mark"—and if she let
Herself be lessoned so, nor plainly set
Her wits to yours, forsooth, and made excuse—
E'en then would be some stooping; and I choose
Never to stoop. Oh, sir, she smiled, no doubt,
Whene'er I passed her; but who passed without
Much the same smile? This grew; I gave commands;
Then all smiles stopped together. There she stands
As if alive. Will't please you rise? We'll meet
The company below, then. I repeat,
The Count your master's known munificence
Is ample warrant that no just pretense
Of mine for dowry will be disallowed;
Though his fair daughter's self, as I avowed
At starting, is my object. Nay, we'll go
Together down, sir. Notice Neptune, though,
Taming a sea-horse, thought a rarity,
Which Claus of Innsbruck cast in bronze for me!

Source: Robert Browning, "My Last Duchess," *Dramatic Lyrics*, 1842.

TEXT STRUCTURE
From "My Last Duchess"

My Last Duchess
by Robert Browning

FERRARA

That's my last Duchess painted on the wall,
Looking as if she were alive. I call
That piece a wonder, now; Fra Pandolf's hands
Worked busily a day, and there she stands.
Will't please you sit and look at her? I said

who is in the picture

"Fra Pandolf" by design, for never read
Strangers like you that pictured countenance,
The depth and passion of its earnest glance,
But to myself they turned (since none puts by
The curtain I have drawn for you, but I)
And seemed as they would ask me, if they durst,
How such a glance came there; so, not the first
Are you to turn and ask thus. Sir, 'twas not

what people want to know (when they look)

Her husband's presence only, called that spot
Of joy into the Duchess' cheek; perhaps
Fra Pandolf chanced to say, "Her mantle laps
Over my lady's wrist too much," or "Paint
Must never hope to reproduce the faint
Half-flush that dies along her throat." Such stuff
Was courtesy, she thought, and cause enough
For calling up that spot of joy. She had

the answer to that question

A heart—how shall I say?— too soon made glad,
Too easily impressed; she liked whate'er
She looked on, and her looks went everywhere.
Sir, 'twas all one! My favour at her breast,
The dropping of the daylight in the West,
The bough of cherries some officious fool
Broke in the orchard for her, the white mule
She rode with round the terrace—all and each

something unique about her

(and what happened to her)

(Continued)

(Continued)

Would draw from her alike the approving speech,
Or blush, at least. She thanked men—good! but thanked
Somehow—I know not how—as if she ranked
My gift of a nine-hundred-years-old name
With anybody's gift. Who'd stoop to blame
This sort of trifling? Even had you skill
In speech—which I have not—to make your will
Quite clear to such an one, and say, "Just this
Or that in you disgusts me; here you miss,
Or there exceed the mark"—and if she let
Herself be lessoned so, nor plainly set
Her wits to yours, forsooth, and made excuse—
E'en then would be some stooping; and I choose
Never to stoop. Oh, sir, she smiled, no doubt,
Whene'er I passed her; but who passed without
Much the same smile? This grew; I gave commands;
Then all smiles stopped together. There she stands
As if alive. Will't please you rise? We'll meet
The company below, then. I repeat,
The Count your master's known munificence
Is ample warrant that no just pretense
Of mine for dowry will be disallowed;
Though his fair daughter's self, as I avowed
At starting, is my object. Nay, we'll go
Together down, sir. Notice Neptune, though,
Taming a sea-horse, thought a rarity,
Which Claus of Innsbruck cast in bronze for me!

what I want to show you next

A Picture that Tells A Story

| Who is in the picture | What people want to Know (when they look) | the answer to that question | Something unique about the Person (and what happened to them) | What I want to Show you next |

Thorns and Thickets

A shadow across his face
With hands folded and tucked under the chin
He closes his eyes in smoky rooms

This early morning gloom
This late-night euphoria
In hushed whispers or clenched teeth
He prays for a salvation which may never come

These holy benedictions spill from lips
Incantations to find a righteous path
Even though he comes from a road of thorns and thickets

His fervency and fears lessen
But sometimes he still finds himself
In dark corners, implorations
Tucked under his tongue

Forgiveness is foreign to him but
In early morning gloom or
Late night euphoria
He closes his eyes
And rests

Jana Jarvis
College Student

WRITE.

1 Freewrite for 3 minutes (then set aside).

Think of a time when plans got ruined.

Write about that.

*Nobody starts with a blank page.

READ.

Notice:
- dialect
- direct address

2 Read the poem. Aloud. Slowly. Read it again, and this time everyone should underline parts they find striking. Discuss the parts they notice. Name the craft. Notice the parts.

GET THE STRUCTURE.

3 Reveal the chunked poem. (Students copy the chunks.) Re-read the poem, watching the movement of the structure.

Ruined Plans

| what bad thing happened accidentally | what you had planned | what happened instead | the truth about plans | one way you're lucky |

WRITE.

4 Invite students to write a poem.
Right now you have
- A page of thoughts
- Examples of craft you like
- A text structure

See what you come up with!
Use any of those, change any, and see what you write in the next minutes.

To a Mouse
On Turning Up in Her Nest With the Plough, November, 1785
by Robert Burns

Wee, sleeket, cowran, tim'rous beastie,
O, what a panic's in thy breastie!
Thou need na start awa sae hasty,
   Wi' bickerin brattle!
I wad be laith to rin an' chase thee
   Wi' murd'ring pattle!

I'm truly sorry Man's dominion
Has broken Nature's social union,
An' justifies that ill opinion,
   Which makes thee startle,
At me, thy poor, earth-born companion,
   An' fellow-mortal!

I doubt na, whyles, but thou may thieve;
What then? poor beastie, thou maun live!
A daimen-icker in a thrave
   'S a sma' request:
I'll get a blessin wi' the lave,
   An' never miss 't!

Thy wee-bit housie, too, in ruin!
It's silly wa's the win's are strewin!
An' naething, now, to big a new ane,
   O' foggage green!
An' bleak December's winds ensuin,
   Baith snell an' keen!

Thou saw the fields laid bare an' waste,
An' weary Winter comin fast,
An' cozie here, beneath the blast,
   Thou thought to dwell,
Till crash! the cruel coulter past
   Out thro' thy cell.

That wee-bit heap o' leaves an' stibble
Has cost thee monie a weary nibble!
Now thou's turn'd out, for a' thy trouble,
   But house or hald,
To thole the Winter's sleety dribble,
   An' cranreuch cauld!

But Mousie, thou art no thy-lane,
In proving foresight may be vain:
The best laid schemes o' Mice an' Men
   Gang aft agley,
An' lea'e us nought but grief an' pain,
   For promis'd joy!

Still, thou art blest, compar'd wi' me!
The present only toucheth thee:
But Och! I backward cast my e'e,
   On prospects drear!
An' forward tho' I canna see,
   I guess an' fear!

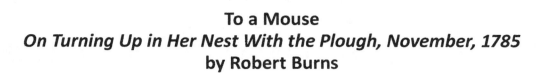

Source: Robert Burns, "To a Mouse," *Poems, Chiefly in the Scottish Dialect,* 1785.

TEXT STRUCTURE
From "To a Mouse"

To a Mouse
On Turning Up in Her Nest With the Plough, November, 1785
by Robert Burns

Wee, sleeket, cowran, tim'rous beastie,
O, what a panic's in thy breastie!
Thou need na start awa sae hasty,
    Wi' bickerin brattle!
I wad be laith to rin an' chase thee
    Wi' murd'ring pattle!

I'm truly sorry Man's dominion
Has broken Nature's social union,
An' justifies that ill opinion,
    Which makes thee startle,
At me, thy poor, earth-born companion,
    An' fellow-mortal!

what bad thing accidentally happened

I doubt na, whyles, but thou may thieve;
What then? poor beastie, thou maun live!
A daimen-icker in a thrave
    'S a sma' request:
I'll get a blessin wi' the lave,
    An' never miss 't!

Thy wee-bit housie, too, in ruin!
It's silly wa's the win's are strewin!
An' naething, now, to big a new ane,
    O' foggage green!
An' bleak December's winds ensuin,
    Baith snell an' keen!

what you were planning

Thou saw the fields laid bare an' waste,
An' weary Winter comin fast,
An' cozie here, beneath the blast,
    Thou thought to dwell,
Till crash! the cruel coulter past
    Out thro' thy cell.

That wee-bit heap o' leaves an' stibble
Has cost thee monie a weary nibble!
Now thou's turn'd out, for a' thy trouble,
    But house or hald,
To thole the Winter's sleety dribble,
    An' cranreuch cauld!

what happened instead

But Mousie, thou art no thy-lane,
In proving foresight may be vain:
The best laid schemes o' Mice an' Men
    Gang aft agley,
An' lea'e us nought but grief an' pain,
    For promis'd joy!

the truth about plans

Still, thou art blest, compar'd wi' me!
The present only toucheth thee:
But Och! I backward cast my e'e,
    On prospects drear!
An' forward tho' I canna see,
    I guess an' fear!

one way you're lucky

Ruined Plans

what bad thing happened accidentally	what you had planned	what happened instead	the truth about plans	one way you're lucky

Thanks a Lot Brother!

I want to go to Founders y'all
please please please.
No your brother has soccer.

Why does he get what he wants
but I don't get what I want?
That is messed up y'all.

I was planning to have three funnel cakes
and ride all of the rides
and taste all of the foods.

But now I am stuck here
watching a boring old soccer game.
But after all, I get to watch him win the tournament!

And at least I got to go to IHOP
and eat all of the pancakes I wanted.

Maren Kraham
Grade 4

Amazing Pancakes

They said to me
fetch some powder for some pancakes
I went in the pantry and
I accidentally got powdered sugar.

I planned on having fluffy
buttery
golden brown
pancakes

instead they were so sweet
that you didn't even need syrup

not golden brown
but white
because of all the powdered sugar.

The truth was
I wanted to make good pancakes
and be one of the
best cooks.

At least I got to
eat really sweet
pancakes and
be with family.

Solomon Igharo
Grade 4

WRITE.

1 Freewrite for 3 minutes (then set aside).

Think about something you did that caused something else.
And you couldn't stop thinking about it.
Write about that.

*Nobody starts with a blank page.

READ.

Notice:
- rhymed couplet
- direct quotes
- iambic tetrameter
- framing with a phrase at beginning and end
- inverted syntax (no language could my grief define)

2 Read the poem. Aloud. Slowly. Read it again, and this time everyone should underline parts they find striking. Discuss the parts they notice. Name the craft. Notice the parts.

GET THE STRUCTURE.

3 Reveal the chunked poem. (Students copy the chunks.) Re-read the poem, watching the movement of the structure.

What I Did That Caused This Feeling

| What I did | how the other person reacted | what happened next | how I felt |

WRITE.

4 Invite students to write a poem.
Right now you have
- A page of thoughts
- Examples of craft you like
- A text structure

See what you come up with!
Use any of those, change any, and see what you write in the next minutes.

Regret
by Olivia Ward Bush-Banks

I said a thoughtless word one day,

A loved one heard and went away;

I cried: "Forgive me, I was blind;

I would not wound or be unkind."

I waited long, but all in vain,

To win my loved one back again.

Too late, alas! to weep and pray,

Death came; my loved one passed away.

Then, what a bitter fate was mine;

No language could my grief define;

Tears of deep regret could not unsay

The thoughtless word I spoke that day.

Source: Olivia Ward Bush-Banks, "Regret."

Regret
by Olivia Ward Bush-Banks

I said a thoughtless word one day,   — *what I did*

A loved one heard and went away;

I cried: "Forgive me, I was blind;   — *how the other person reacted*

I would not wound or be unkind."

I waited long, but all in vain,

To win my loved one back again.

Too late, alas! to weep and pray,   — *what happened next*

Death came; my loved one passed away.

Then, what a bitter fate was mine;   — *how I felt*

No language could my grief define;

Tears of deep regret could not unsay

The thoughtless word I spoke that day.

What I Did That Caused This Feeling

| What I did | how the other person reacted | what happened next | how I felt |

I Wish

"I hope you die." I wish I didn't say
those words to you, Dad.
Of all of the words I said, I didn't say "I love you."

Our bond had fallen apart
like a broken glass, shattered to pieces.

The love I had for you was still there,
but lost like Peter Pan.

Please forgive me.

I didn't know your day would come so soon.
I thought I would be able to talk to you again.

But you died.

**Beautiful Williams
Grade 8**

For Granted

I never paid attention when you asked me to help you
in the garden where you grew roses, grapefruits,
and the Chinese plum tree. I didn't want to. I was 8.

But you loved me. I thought we'd have more time.

We were on our way to your house, but
you passed away before we could get there.

Now I wish I could help you around the house
water your plants, pull weeds.

**Nicholas Herrera
Grade 8**

WRITE.

1 Freewrite for 3 minutes (then set aside).

Choose one important moment in your life and write down everything you can remember.

*Nobody starts with a blank page.

READ.

Notice:
- the dashes
- strange capitals
- the idea of a disruption

2 Read the poem. Aloud. Slowly. Read it again, and this time everyone should underline parts they find striking. Discuss the parts they notice. Name the craft. Notice the parts.

GET THE STRUCTURE.

3 Reveal the chunked poem. (Students copy the chunks.) Re-read the poem, watching the movement of the structure.

the Moment When Something Important Happened

| what the place felt like | what the other people were doing | what had already happened | the unexpected thing that happened |

WRITE.

4 Invite students to write a poem. Right now you have
- A page of thoughts
- Examples of craft you like
- A text structure

See what you come up with!
Use any of those, change any, and see what you write in the next minutes.

I Heard a Fly Buzz - When I Died
by Emily Dickinson

I heard a Fly buzz - when I died -
The Stillness in the Room
Was like the Stillness in the Air -
Between the Heaves of Storm -

The Eyes around - had wrung them dry -
And Breaths were gathering firm
For that last Onset - when the King
Be witnessed - in the Room -

I willed my Keepsakes - Signed away
What portion of me be
Assignable - and then it was
There interposed a Fly -

With Blue - uncertain - stumbling Buzz -
Between the light - and me -
And then the Windows failed - and then
I could not see to see -

Source: Emily Dickinson, "I Heard a Fly Buzz - When I Died," *Poems by Emily Dickinson*, Roberts Brothers, 1896.

I Heard a Fly Buzz - When I Died
by Emily Dickinson

I heard a Fly buzz - when I died -
The Stillness in the Room
Was like the Stillness in the Air -
Between the Heaves of Storm -

what the place felt like

The Eyes around - had wrung them dry -
And Breaths were gathering firm
For that last Onset - when the King
Be witnessed - in the Room -

what people were doing

I willed my Keepsakes - Signed away
What portion of me be
Assignable - and then it was
There interposed a Fly -

what had already happened

With Blue - uncertain - stumbling Buzz -
Between the light - and me -
And then the Windows failed - and then
I could not see to see -

the unexpected thing that happened

The Moment When Something Important Happened

| what the place felt like | what the other people were doing | what had already happened | the unexpected thing that happened |

A Childhood Keepsake

Lucy is a pre-teen who is in her mom's childhood room.

My mom's room is bright even though it feels dark and as if it is trapping me in. Grandma watches me silently from the door frame as I search for something that would remind me of her, just one keepsake. I already knew that Mom was gone, but I hope that she will appear right in front of me. I'm ready to give up, but I look in one of her drawers and find a false bottom. I lift it up and see all her diaries and a glimmer of something from the corner of my eye. I dig until I see it, a necklace, *her necklace*. I show it to grandma, and she says I can keep it. I am overwhelmed with joy. I finally have something to remind me of her.

Alex Phillips
Grade 7

I Heard a Bell Ring

Behind the school - Next to
the dumpsters -
The hot air dusted my cheeks -
Sounds of people laughing
And shouting -

The Others just stood - watching in
Silence - their eyes squinting -
From the scorching sun - sweat
Dripping from their temples -

It was past the time where
I tried to get away - away from his words -
Enough running.
Raising my hand -
Nails digging into palm -
And then it was -

A ringing sound - a bell -
A dismissal of my
Clenched fist
And him

Emi Ramirez
Grade 8

31

WRITE.

1 Freewrite for 3 minutes (then set aside).

Think of a time when there was something (even something trivial) that was meaningful to you, and you were saving it. But someone else ruined it, destroyed it, ate it, lost it, drew on it.
Write about that.

*Nobody starts with a blank page.

READ.

Notice:
- hard rhymes (thee, be)
- Slant rhymes (this, is)
- narrative feature (She killed the flea?!)

2 Read the poem. Aloud. Slowly.
Read it again, and this time everyone should underline parts they find striking. Discuss the parts they notice. Name the craft. Notice the parts.

GET THE STRUCTURE.

3 Reveal the chunked poem. (Students copy the chunks.) Re-read the poem, watching the movement of the structure.

You Ruined My (object)

| Describe the thing | Why it mattered to me | Who messed with it | What they gained from it |

WRITE.

4 Invite students to write a poem.
Right now you have
- A page of thoughts
- Examples of craft you like
- A text structure

See what you come up with!
Use any of those, change any, and see what you write in the next minutes.

The Flea
by John Donne

Mark but this flea, and mark in this,
How little that which thou deniest me is;
It sucked me first, and now sucks thee,
And in this flea our two bloods mingled be;
Thou know'st that this cannot be said
A sin, nor shame, nor loss of maidenhead,
   Yet this enjoys before it woo,
    And pampered swells with one blood made of two,
    And this, alas, is more than we would do.

Oh stay, three lives in one flea spare,
Where we almost, nay more than married are.
This flea is you and I, and this
Our marriage bed, and marriage temple is;
Though parents grudge, and you, w'are met,
And cloistered in these living walls of jet.
   Though use make you apt to kill me,
   Let not to that, self-murder added be,
   And sacrilege, three sins in killing three.

Cruel and sudden, hast thou since
Purpled thy nail, in blood of innocence?
Wherein could this flea guilty be,
Except in that drop which it sucked from thee?
Yet thou triumph'st, and say'st that thou
Find'st not thy self, nor me the weaker now;
   'Tis true; then learn how false, fears be:
   Just so much honor, when thou yield'st to me,
   Will waste, as this flea's death took life from thee.

Source: John Donne, "The Flea," 1633.

TEXT STRUCTURE
From "The Flea"

The Flea
by John Donne

Mark but this flea, and mark in this,
How little that which thou deniest me is;
It sucked me first, and now sucks thee,
And in this flea our two bloods mingled be;
Thou know'st that this cannot be said
A sin, nor shame, nor loss of maidenhead,
    Yet this enjoys before it woo,
    And pampered swells with one blood made of two,
    And this, alas, is more than we would do.

description of the thing

Oh stay, three lives in one flea spare,
Where we almost, nay more than married are.
This flea is you and I, and this
Our marriage bed, and marriage temple is;
Though parents grudge, and you, w'are met,
And cloistered in these living walls of jet.
    Though use make you apt to kill me,
    Let not to that, self-murder added be,
    And sacrilege, three sins in killing three.

why it matters to me

Cruel and sudden, hast thou since
Purpled thy nail, in blood of innocence?
Wherein could this flea guilty be,
Except in that drop which it sucked from thee?
Yet thou triumph'st, and say'st that thou
Find'st not thy self, nor me the weaker now;

who messed with it

what they gained from it

    'Tis true; then learn how false, fears be:
    Just so much honor, when thou yield'st to me,
    Will waste, as this flea's death took life from thee.

You Ruined My (object)

| Describe the thing | Why it mattered to me | Who messed with it | What they gained from it |

The Pictures

They were pictures of the ocean—
My dad's favorite place.
 I could hear his voice: "You can do anything there."

About three years ago,
I lost him.
Liver cancer.
His hazel eyes loved the blinding ocean.

About a year after he passed
everyone close to my dad took a trip to Florida.
Cocoa Beach.

I carried the love he had
and captured the moment with my eyes.
I took pictures of the view
for my dad
of the beautiful water
and printed them.

The moment was ruined.
My cousin
little Bianca put down her red drink,
bumped and spilled it,
hid the ruined and wet pictures from me.
My heart dropped when I saw.
I suffered, anger in my eyes.

She gained nothing but sorrow
and cried.

Alexis Ramirez
Grade 8

WRITE.

1 Freewrite for 3 minutes (then set aside).

Think of Something you heard-- a Sound that you remember-- a Sound that captured your attention or imagination.

Write about that.

*Nobody starts with a blank page.

READ.

Notice:
- Contrasts (outside/in)
- hymn meter
  [iambic tetrameter + iambic trimeter]
- Simile

2 Read the poem. Aloud. Slowly. Read it again, and this time everyone should underline parts they find striking. Discuss the parts they notice. Name the craft. Notice the parts.

GET THE STRUCTURE.

3 Reveal the chunked poem. (Students copy the chunks.) Re-read the poem, watching the movement of the structure.

A Sound

| Outside what the weather was like | what all was going on | what sound I zoomed in on | what it reminded me of |

WRITE.

4 Invite students to write a poem. Right now you have
- A page of thoughts
- Examples of craft you like
- A text structure

See what you come up with!
Use any of those, change any, and see what you write in the next minutes.

A Musical
by Paul Lawrence Dunbar

Outside the rain upon the street,
   The sky all grim of hue,
Inside, the music – painful sweet,
   And yet I heard but you.

As is a thrilling violin,
   So is your voice to me,
And still above the other strains,
   It sang in ecstasy.

Source: Paul Laurence Dunbar, "A Musical," *The Complete Poems of Paul Laurence Dunbar*, Dodd, Mead and Company, 1913.

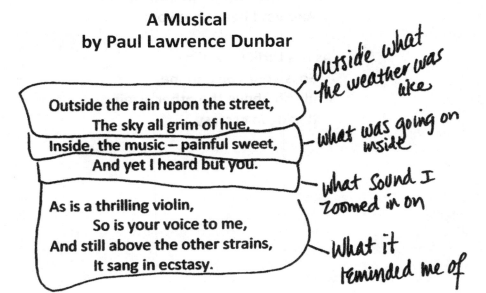

A Musical
by Paul Lawrence Dunbar

Outside the rain upon the street,
  The sky all grim of hue,
Inside, the music — painful sweet,
  And yet I heard but you.

As is a thrilling violin,
  So is your voice to me,
And still above the other strains,
  It sang in ecstasy.

Outside what the weather was like

what was going on inside

what sound I zoomed in on

What it reminded me of

A Sound

| Outside what the weather was like | what all was going on | What sound I zoomed in on | what it reminded me of |

The Call

The sky was baby blue,
and the sun was shining bright.
Yet, inside was a terrible storm
destroying everything in its path.

In the distance I heard a bird
calling to another from afar.
I thought of you,
how your voice always brought me back.

Eris Carvajal
Grade 10

Inside

Inside the son burns with rage,
for he is covered in chains,
for he has only known his cage,
and has been seared with pain.

A door has opened within the cage.
A sweet voice sang.
The son began a new page
and sang in thanks.

Ethan Nieto
Grade 10

WRITE.

1 Freewrite for 3 minutes (then set aside).

> Write about your neighborhood.

*Nobody starts with a blank page.

READ.

> Notice:
> · Sensory details
> · personification

2 Read the poem. Aloud. Slowly. Read it again, and this time everyone should underline parts they find striking. Discuss the parts they notice. Name the craft. Notice the parts.

GET THE STRUCTURE.

3 Reveal the chunked poem. (Students copy the chunks.) Re-read the poem, watching the movement of the structure.

> At This Time of Day
>
> | What time and what season it is | What you can see (or feel) from where you stand | What you can see a little farther away | one thing that happens every day at this time |

WRITE.

4 Invite students to write a poem. Right now you have
- A page of thoughts
- Examples of craft you like
- A text structure

See what you come up with!
Use any of those, change any, and see what you write in the next minutes.

Preludes (Excerpt)
by T.S. Eliot

I.
The winter evening settles down
With smell of steaks in passageways.
Six o'clock.
The burnt-out ends of smoky days.
And now a gusty shower wraps
The grimy scraps
Of withered leaves about your feet
And newspapers from vacant lots;
The showers beat
On broken blinds and chimney-pots,
And at the corner of the street
A lonely cab-horse steams and stamps.

And then the lighting of the lamps.

Source: T.S. Eliot, "Preludes," *Prufrock and Other Observations*, 1917.

TEXT STRUCTURE
From "Preludes" (Excerpt)

Preludes (Excerpt)
by T.S. Eliot

I.

The winter evening settles down
With smell of steaks in passageways.
Six o'clock.

what time it is

The burnt-out ends of smoky days.
And now a gusty shower wraps
The grimy scraps
Of withered leaves about your feet
And newspapers from vacant lots;
The showers beat
On broken blinds and chimney-pots,

what you can see

And at the corner of the street
A lonely cab-horse steams and stamps.

farther away

And then the lighting of the lamps.

happens every day at this time

At This Time of Day

What time and what season it is	What you can see (or feel) from where you stand	What you can see a little farther away	one thing that happens every day at this time

Fall Is Now in Control

It's a Sunday at 5 o'clock.
I walk around the park and see
some kids playing basketball.

I walk more and smell
the oozing smell
of food. I try to ignore it, so

I walk the other way.
When I feel comfortable
some random dog jumps
out of nowhere, and completely

makes me go crying home.
Every step I take, I hear
the crunch of leaves,

but I don't let that take me away
from going home.

Andy Martinez
Grade 6

Summer Evening

The summer evening settles down
with the smell of salt and ocean breeze.
7 o'clock
the soft white sand and palm trees.
And now a teal wave crashes
and water splashes
on visitors from everywhere
and sea creatures in the night.
I feel the water in my hair
and ocean dew in the air.
Then I look toward the big orange light
and I see a chair
as if just sitting, waiting for me.

I sit down next to the big, blue sea.

Ryan Arredondo
Grade 7

WRITE.

1 Freewrite for 3 minutes (then set aside).

Make a list of things people disagree about (flavors of ice cream, staying or going, etc.)

See how many you can list, in 2 minutes.

*Nobody starts with a blank page.

READ.

Notice:
- not a usual rhyme scheme
- repeated sounds

2 Read the poem. Aloud. Slowly.
Read it again, and this time everyone should underline parts they find striking. Discuss the parts they notice. Name the craft. Notice the parts.

GET THE STRUCTURE.

3 Reveal the chunked poem. (Students copy the chunks.) Re-read the poem, watching the movement of the structure.

My Response to a Disagreement

| two points of view | how I agree with the first one | but how I also agree with the second one |

WRITE.

4 Invite students to write a poem.
Right now you have
- A page of thoughts
- Examples of craft you like
- A text structure

See what you come up with!
Use any of those, change any, and see what you write in the next minutes.

Fire and Ice
by Robert Frost

Some say the world will end in fire,
Some say in ice.
From what I've tasted of desire
I hold with those who favor fire.
But if it had to perish twice,
I think I know enough of hate
To say that for destruction ice
Is also great
And would suffice.

Source: Robert Frost, "Fire and Ice," *New Hampshire*, Henry Holt, 1913.

**Fire and Ice
by Robert Frost**

Some say the world will end in fire,
Some say in ice.

two points of view

From what I've tasted of desire
I hold with those who favor fire.

how I agree with the first one

But if it had to perish twice,
I think I know enough of hate
To say that for destruction ice
Is also great
And would suffice.

but how I also partly agree with the second

My Response to a Disagreement

| two points of view | how I agree with the first one | but how I also agree with the second one |

Toothpaste

My brother and I like to brush our teeth,
but we share the same sink.
It's crazy to think,
but the toothpaste is always dirty.
He declares it is my fault,
of course it never is,
for I am nice and tidy.
My dad always wonders out loud,
"Why, who did this?"
I always point at him.
He points at me.
So I guess we'll never know
who the real toothpaster is
(even if we all know who it really is).

Isabella Frerich
Grade 5

Sun and Rain

Some say the shine is better
Some say the rain
From what I've seen
I will always favor the shine.
If I could have both, I would
But I'd rather let the sun shine.

Kaylee Phelps
Grade 7

The Best Texas Team

Some say the Spurs are superior
Some say the Rockets

From what I've observed in this thriller,
The Spurs are plainly better

However, the Rockets
Have a better record,
So it may seem as if
They aren't inferior

Sarah Stefoni
Grade 7

WRITE.

1 Freewrite for 3 minutes (then set aside).

Think of a time in history when something changed. Imagine how someone's life might change, how life would be different. Write about that.

*Nobody starts with a blank page.

READ.

Notice:
- hymn meter
- rhyme scheme
  ABCB
- fictional narrator
  Narrator (Chloe) tells the story, not the poet (Frances)

2 Read the poem.
Aloud. Slowly.
Read it again, and this time everyone should underline parts they find striking. Discuss the parts they notice. Name the craft. Notice the parts.

GET THE STRUCTURE.

3 Reveal the chunked poem. (Students copy the chunks.) Re-read the poem, watching the movement of the structure.

the Story of A Moment In History

| the new thing that is happening | how things used to be different | the new thing | what this meant I could do now | what people said | what I did about it |

WRITE.

4 Invite students to write a poem.
Right now you have
- A page of thoughts
- Examples of craft you like
- A text structure

See what you come up with!
Use any of those, change any, and see what you write in the next minutes.

Learning to Read
by Frances Ellen Harper

Very soon the Yankee teachers
    Came down and set up school;
But, oh! how the Rebs did hate it,—
    It was agin' their rule.

Our masters always tried to hide
    Book learning from our eyes;
Knowledge didn't agree with slavery—
    'Twould make us all too wise.

But some of us would try to steal
    A little from the book.
And put the words together,
    And learn by hook or crook.

I remember Uncle Caldwell,
    Who took pot liquor fat
And greased the pages of his book,
    And hid it in his hat.

And had his master ever seen
    The leaves upon his head,
He'd have thought them greasy papers,
    But nothing to be read.

And there was Mr. Turner's Ben,
    Who heard the children spell,
And picked the words right up by heart,
    And learned to read 'em well.

Well, the Northern folks kept sending
    The Yankee teachers down;
And they stood right up and helped us,
    Though Rebs did sneer and frown.

And I longed to read my Bible,
    For precious words it said;
But when I begun to learn it,
    Folks just shook their heads,

And said there is no use trying,
    Oh! Chloe, you're too late;
But as I was rising sixty,
    I had no time to wait.

So I got a pair of glasses,
    And straight to work I went,
And never stopped till I could read
    The hymns and Testament.

Then I got a little cabin
    A place to call my own—
And I felt independent
    As the queen upon her throne.

Source: Frances Ellen Harper, "Learning to Read."

35

Learning to Read
by Frances Ellen Harper

Very soon the Yankee teachers
  Came down and set up school;
But, oh! how the Rebs did hate it,—
  It was agin' their rule.

the new thing that is happening

Our masters always tried to hide
  Book learning from our eyes;
Knowledge didn't agree with slavery—
  'Twould make us all too wise.

But some of us would try to steal
  A little from the book.
And put the words together,
  And learn by hook or crook.

I remember Uncle Caldwell,
  Who took pot liquor fat
And greased the pages of his book,
  And hid it in his hat.

And had his master ever seen
  The leaves upon his head,
He'd have thought them greasy papers,
  But nothing to be read.

And there was Mr. Turner's Ben,
  Who heard the children spell,
And picked the words right up by heart,
  And learned to read 'em well.

how things used to be different

Well, the Northern folks kept sending
  The Yankee teachers down;
And they stood right up and helped us,
  Though Rebs did sneer and frown.

the new thing

And I longed to read my Bible,
  For precious words it said;
But when I begun to learn it,
  Folks just shook their heads,

what this meant I could do now

And said there is no use trying,
  Oh! Chloe, you're too late;
But as I was rising sixty,
  I had no time to wait.

What people said

So I got a pair of glasses,
  And straight to work I went,
And never stopped till I could read
  The hymns and Testament.

Then I got a little cabin
  A place to call my own—
And I felt independent
  As the queen upon her throne.

what I did about it

the Story of A Moment In History

| the new thing that is happening | how things used to be different | the new thing | what this meant I could do now | what people said | what I did about it |

The Preacher's Wrath

Thick dust
Stretches its arms across the fields.
As if it were a swarm of mosquitos,
Trampling the weak corn stalks.
The land is one plain of cream.
A blizzard of drying powder.
Children bury their faces in their mother's aprons.
Pigs screech,
Dust filled streets,
Cannot bear the heat,
Piles at their feet.

Every highway has a crowd of trucks.
Passengers dreaming of the West and
Drivers shaking their heads.
Grandpa sneers ahead,
For he regrets.
He left himself, along with
Centuries of family history.
Home is not West.

Storefronts and gas stations eagerly await.
Money, money, money.
Not enough to have a ceremony for grandpa.
We have to bury him ourselves.
Not enough to fix our automobile.
We have to scrounge in the junkyard.
Gas, food, shelter.
Dust, dust, dust.

Papa wants to smoke a pipe.
Clouds of dust fill his lungs instead.
The four mattresses almost slide off the truck.
Two chickens begin to rally up
The dog.
Family of eight trudge in one truck
In the dusty air under the
Scorching sun.

Momma's teary eyes are locked ahead.
She's bundled up with her family,
But feels as though she has lost them.
Brother chatters about the grape fields.
Auntie imagines picking oranges.
Grandma shivers and prays.
Nobody has noticed that
There isn't a preacher anymore.

Jessie Clyne
Grade 12

TEACHING NOTES
for "Old Ironsides"

WRITE.

1 Freewrite for 3 minutes (then set aside).

> Think about a time when someone tried to impose a new rule. And you thought was a bad idea.
>
> Describe that time.

*Nobody starts with a blank page.

READ.

Notice:
- Sarcasm
- direct address
- response to a current event
- hymn meter
- classical allusion
- personification (harpy)
- Biblical allusion (nail that...)

2 Read the poem. Aloud. Slowly.
Read it again, and this time everyone should underline parts they find striking. Discuss the parts they notice. Name the craft. Notice the parts.

GET THE STRUCTURE.

3 Reveal the chunked poem. (Students copy the chunks.) Re-read the poem, watching the movement of the structure.

Reaction to A Bad Idea

| what the bad idea is (for change) | how things have worked well before | the good results we have had | a better way to handle it |

WRITE.

4 Invite students to write a poem.
Right now you have
- A page of thoughts
- Examples of craft you like
- A text structure

See what you come up with!
Use any of those, change any, and see what you write in the next minutes.

Old Ironsides
by Oliver Wendell Holmes

Ay, tear her tattered ensign down!
   Long has it waved on high,
And many an eye has danced to see
   That banner in the sky;
Beneath it rung the battle shout,
   And burst the cannon's roar;—
The meteor of the ocean air
   Shall sweep the clouds no more!

Her deck, once red with heroes' blood
   Where knelt the vanquished foe,
When winds were hurrying o'er the flood
   And waves were white below,
No more shall feel the victor's tread,
   Or know the conquered knee;—
The harpies of the shore shall pluck
   The eagle of the sea!

O, better that her shattered hulk
   Should sink beneath the wave;
Her thunders shook the mighty deep,
   And there should be her grave;
Nail to the mast her holy flag,
   Set every thread-bare sail,
And give her to the god of storms,—
   The lightning and the gale!

Source: Oliver Wendell Holmes, "Old Ironsides," *Advertiser,* 1830.

Old Ironsides
by Oliver Wendell Holmes

Ay, tear her tattered ensign down!
    Long has it waved on high,
And many an eye has danced to see
    That banner in the sky;
Beneath it rung the battle shout,
    And burst the cannon's roar;—
The meteor of the ocean air
    Shall sweep the clouds no more!

— *your bad idea*

— *how well things have worked before*

Her deck, once red with heroes' blood
    Where knelt the vanquished foe,
When winds were hurrying o'er the flood
    And waves were white below,
No more shall feel the victor's tread,
    Or know the conquered knee;—
The harpies of the shore shall pluck
    The eagle of the sea!

— *the good results we've had*

O, better that her shattered hulk
    Should sink beneath the wave;
Her thunders shook the mighty deep,
    And there should be her grave;
Nail to the mast her holy flag,
    Set every thread-bare sail,
And give her to the god of storms,—
    The lightning and the gale!

— *a better way to handle this*

Reaction to A Bad Idea

what the bad idea is (for change)	how things have worked well before	the good results we have had	a better way to handle it

Middle School Move

Yeah, let's just move to the center of the Sahara. It feels essentially like the same thing.

We have been doing fine in Illinois. All three of us sisters have spent
almost all of our lives under this roof. We danced around the rectangle rug,
singing to Aretha Franklin. I had plans to change my bright pink room
into a crisp white, mature enough for a high schooler.

The halls, once full of laughter, now sit quiet and still, and the walls have all been
slathered with the boring Almond Beige. We would bounce the tennis ball off
the door of the garage, and do cannonballs into the neighbor's pool. This was
the place where my sister was born, and on that same day, my grandparents
fed us five gallons of popcorn and we watched Willy Wonka eight times in a row.

Why do we have to uproot our lives here? Why can't Dad just quit and get another
job instead of being relocated across the country? Why does it have to
be *Texas*? Y'all can keep your boots and Big Red. Let's just keep our house
here in this city, and let me continue to high school with my friends. Don't make me go.

Essie Gross
Grade 7

WRITE.

1 Freewrite for 3 minutes (then set aside).

There are some things that most people agree are beautiful, but what are some strange or unusual things that you find to be beautiful or wonderful?

*Nobody starts with a blank page.

READ.

Notice:
- rhymed curtal (shortened) sonnet
- alliteration
- enumeration (listing/pitchforking)
- rhyme scheme
- hyphenated words

2 Read the poem. Aloud. Slowly. Read it again, and this time everyone should underline parts they find striking. Discuss the parts they notice. Name the craft. Notice the parts.

GET THE STRUCTURE.

3 Reveal the chunked poem. (Students copy the chunks.) Re-read the poem, watching the movement of the structure.

Praise Poem

I give thanks for things that ___

the things that are ___ (a list)

I sing your praises

WRITE.

4 Invite students to write a poem. Right now you have
- A page of thoughts
- Examples of craft you like
- A text structure

See what you come up with!
Use any of those, change any, and see what you write in the next minutes.

Pied Beauty
by Gerard Manley Hopkins

Glory be to God for dappled things –

    For skies of couple-colour as a brinded cow;

        For rose-moles all in stipple upon trout that swim;

Fresh-firecoal chestnut-falls; finches' wings;

    Landscape plotted and pieced – fold, fallow, and plough;

        And áll trádes, their gear and tackle and trim.

All things counter, original, spare, strange;

    Whatever is fickle, freckled (who knows how?)

        With swift, slow; sweet, sour; adazzle, dim;

He fathers-forth whose beauty is past change:

        Praise him.

Source: Gerard Manley Hopkins, "Pied Beauty," *Poems of Gerard Manley Hopkins*, 1918.

Pied Beauty
by Gerard Manley Hopkins

Glory be to God for dappled things —

I give thanks for things that are ___. (patchy or blemished)

For skies of couple-colour as a brinded cow;

For rose-moles all in stipple upon trout that swim;

Fresh-firecoal chestnut-falls; finches' wings;

Landscape plotted and pieced — fold, fallow, and plough;

And áll trádes, their gear and tackle and trim.

the things that are ___ (a list)

All things counter, original, spare, strange;

Whatever is fickle, freckled (who knows how?)

With swift, slow; sweet, sour; adazzle, dim;

He fathers-forth whose beauty is past change:

Praise him.

I sing your praises.

Praise Poem

| I give thanks for things that ___ | the things that are ___ (a list) | I sing your praises |

In Reverence

I call upon the muses to sing in ancient languages
Of rust and stone

To sing of the splendor found in—
    A withered butterfly wing
    Blemishes on the moon's face
    Dusty books—their spines giving out from the burden they carry
    Tear stains on the pillow next to me—where you once slept but now the absence is a phantom pain

Sing these sublime songs, muses
In ancient languages of rust and stone

Jana Jarvis
College Student

WRITE.

1 Freewrite for 3 minutes (then set aside).

Think of a time someone gave you advice and you wish you had taken it.

Tell about that.

*Nobody starts with a blank page.

READ.

Notice:
- rhyme
- dialogue
- repetition at the end
- details (crowns and pounds, signifying value

2 Read the poem. Aloud. Slowly. Read it again, and this time everyone should underline parts they find striking. Discuss the parts they notice. Name the craft. Notice the parts.

GET THE STRUCTURE.

3 Reveal the chunked poem. (Students copy the chunks.) Re-read the poem, watching the movement of the structure.

Change of Attitude

| advice someone gave me | what I thought about it then | more advice I was given | what I think about it now |

WRITE.

4 Invite students to write a poem. Right now you have
- A page of thoughts
- Examples of craft you like
- A text structure

See what you come up with!
Use any of those, change any, and see what you write in the next minutes.

When I Was One-and-Twenty
by A. E. Housman

When I was one-and-twenty
   I heard a wise man say,
"Give crowns and pounds and guineas
   But not your heart away;
Give pearls away and rubies
   But keep your fancy free."
But I was one-and-twenty,
   No use to talk to me.

When I was one-and-twenty
   I heard him say again,
"The heart out of the bosom
   Was never given in vain;
'Tis paid with sighs a plenty
   And sold for endless rue."
And I am two-and-twenty,
   And oh, 'tis true, 'tis true.

Source: A. E. Housman, "When I Was One-and-Twenty," *A Shropshire Lad*, 1896.

When I Was One-and-Twenty
by A. E. Housman

When I was one-and-twenty
    I heard a wise man say,
"Give crowns and pounds and guineas
    But not your heart away;
Give pearls away and rubies
    But keep your fancy free."

advice someone gave me

But I was one-and-twenty,
    No use to talk to me.

what I thought about it then

When I was one-and-twenty
    I heard him say again,
"The heart out of the bosom
    Was never given in vain;
'Tis paid with sighs a plenty
    And sold for endless rue."

more advice I was given

And I am two-and-twenty,
    And oh, 'tis true, 'tis true.

what I think about it now

Change of Attitude

advice someone gave me	what I thought about it then	more advice I was given	what I think about it now

Fire!

Before I mixed the two solutions
my mother shouted to me,
"You don't know anything about them,
It could cause a problem."
Like, it could set fire to me.

But I didn't really care.
"No," said the rebel in me.

Before I mixed the two solutions,
I heard mom shout again,
"Before you mix the unknown liquids,
Think is this really the best decision?
Because it's not that good to me."

Now that I recall that,
I can see that it was a fire burning in me,
a fire burning in me.

Keira McAlester
Grade 4

Advice

Once a wise woman said to me:
"Don't end up like me, don't starve yourself."

A few words changed my mood.
A few words changed my attitude.
Those few words were: "You're fat!"
And I believed them.

I then realized how this wise woman *became* wise.

She said,
And looked me in the eye:
"Kyra Grace, you're the reason I'm still alive."
"So don't listen to the negative things people say to you,
they're just jealous
and being foolish."
Just simply foolish.

Kyra Tilley
Grade 4

Advice

When I was nine I was shooting with my rifle,
a man came up to me and said make sure to aim,
and if you don't do not blame.
I didn't listen, of course. I didn't but tried not to make an incident.

But again he says make sure to aim,
and don't you blame.
Now I was ten,
and I listened,
and he was right. You want to aim.

Tucker Lundin
Grade 4

TEACHING NOTES
for "A Jelly-Fish"

1 Freewrite for 3 minutes (then set aside).

Think of something you really wanted, something you didn't get. Write about that.

*Nobody starts with a blank page.

READ.

Notice:
- the contrasts
- enjambment rhyme/disrupted
- images
- repetition
- rhythmic opposites

2 Read the poem. Aloud. Slowly. Read it again, and this time everyone should underline parts they find striking. Discuss the parts they notice. Name the craft. Notice the parts.

GET THE STRUCTURE.

3 Reveal the chunked poem. (Students copy the chunks.) Re-read the poem, watching the movement of the structure.

the thing that Got Away

| describe what you wanted | what happens when you try to get it | then what happens | how it gets away |

WRITE.

4 Invite students to write a poem.
Right now you have
- A page of thoughts
- Examples of craft you like
- A text structure

See what you come up with!
Use any of those, change any, and see what you write in the next minutes.

A Jelly-Fish
by Marianne Moore

Visible, invisible,
A fluctuating charm,
An amber-colored amethyst
Inhabits it; your arm
Approaches, and
It opens and
It closes;
You have meant
To catch it,
And it shrivels;
You abandon
Your intent—
It opens, and it
Closes and you
Reach for it—
The blue
Surrounding it
Grows cloudy, and
It floats away
From you.

Source: Marianne Moore, "A Jelly-Fish," *The Lantern*, 1909.

A Jelly-Fish
by Marianne Moore

Visible, invisible,
A fluctuating charm,
An amber-colored amethyst
Inhabits it; your arm
Approaches, and
It opens and
It closes;
You have meant
To catch it,
And it shrivels;
You abandon
Your intent—
It opens, and it
Closes and you
Reach for it—
The blue
Surrounding it
Grows cloudy, and
It floats away
From you.

Describe what you wanted

What happens when you try to get it

And then what happens

How it gets away

The Thing that Got Away

| describe what you wanted | what happens when you try to get it | then what happens | how it gets away |

Go-Kart Track

Fast, slow
an exhilarating opportunity.
Asphalt colored black
a large, circular track
denied over and over,
I keep trying.
But my parents don't seem to buy it.
I'm not sure why,
but I guess parents just don't abide
to what kids like to buy.
They tell me no, no, no,
but I'm not sure how to show
that I'll be safe and not get thrown.
Safety, oh boy.
And it's too much money, darn.
Why does the H.O.A. have to be so picky
and make our situations so sticky?
Well, slim chance I'll ever get it,
so why try to bend it.

Colton Inglish
Grade 4

A Dog

a fluffy soft
piece of joy
to greet you
every day
a golden colored ball of joy
that approaches you
as you play
it could be small, tall
rough or smooth
I would love it no matter what

I watch my dream slip away
as I get a little fake dog instead

Maren Kraham
Grade 4

Fish

Sitting or standing,
a silver and blackish mess.
I swim as slow as a sloth
but it turns its head.
I stop and it looks away,
so I approach again.
Then it goes under a rock. I need a breath.
I catch my breath and move the rock.
I see it and it sees me.
I dive for it,
but only get to feel its rough scales before
it's gone.

Tyler Rooney
Grade 7

WRITE.

1 Freewrite for 3 minutes (then set aside).

Think of a time when someone told you something would be a certain way, but what you saw was **not** what you expected. Write about that.

*Nobody starts with a blank page.

READ.

Notice:
- alternating rhyme
- grotesque images
- persuasive techniques
- irony
- Latin (allusion to Horace's "it is sweet and fitting to die for one's country.")

2 Read the poem. Aloud. Slowly.
Read it again, and this time everyone should underline parts they find striking. Discuss the parts they notice. Name the craft. Notice the parts.

GET THE STRUCTURE.

3 Reveal the chunked poem. (Students copy the chunks.) Re-read the poem, watching the movement of the structure.

A Truism That's Just Not True

| what we were doing | what happened next | how it has haunted me | what I can't unsee | the saying that is <u>not</u> true |

WRITE.

4 Invite students to write a poem.
Right now you have
- A page of thoughts
- Examples of craft you like
- A text structure

See what you come up with!
Use any of those, change any, and see what you write in the next minutes.

Dulce et Decorum Est
by Wilfred Owen

Bent double, like old beggars under sacks,
Knock-kneed, coughing like hags, we cursed through sludge,
Till on the haunting flares we turned our backs,
And towards our distant rest began to trudge.
Men marched asleep. Many had lost their boots,
But limped on, blood-shod. All went lame; all blind;
Drunk with fatigue; deaf even to the hoots
Of gas-shells dropping softly behind.

Gas! GAS! Quick, boys!—An ecstasy of fumbling
Fitting the clumsy helmets just in time,
But someone still was yelling out and stumbling
And flound'ring like a man in fire or lime.—
Dim through the misty panes and thick green light,
As under a green sea, I saw him drowning.

In all my dreams before my helpless sight,
He plunges at me, guttering, choking, drowning.

If in some smothering dreams, you too could pace
Behind the wagon that we flung him in,
And watch the white eyes writhing in his face,
His hanging face, like a devil's sick of sin;
If you could hear, at every jolt, the blood
Come gargling from the froth-corrupted lungs,
Obscene as cancer, bitter as the cud
Of vile, incurable sores on innocent tongues,—
My friend, you would not tell with such high zest
To children ardent for some desperate glory,
The old Lie: *Dulce et decorum est*
Pro patria mori.

Source: Wilfred Owen, "Dulce et Decorum Est," 1920.

Dulce et Decorum Est
by Wilfred Owen

Bent double, like old beggars under sacks,
Knock-kneed, coughing like hags, we cursed through sludge,
Till on the haunting flares we turned our backs,
And towards our distant rest began to trudge.
Men marched asleep. Many had lost their boots,
But limped on, blood-shod. All went lame; all blind;
Drunk with fatigue; deaf even to the hoots
Of gas-shells dropping softly behind.

what we were doing

Gas! GAS! Quick, boys!—An ecstasy of fumbling
Fitting the clumsy helmets just in time,
But someone still was yelling out and stumbling
And flound'ring like a man in fire or lime.—
Dim through the misty panes and thick green light,
As under a green sea, I saw him drowning.

what happened next

In all my dreams before my helpless sight,
He plunges at me, guttering, choking, drowning.

how it has haunted me

If in some smothering dreams, you too could pace
Behind the wagon that we flung him in,
And watch the white eyes writhing in his face,
His hanging face, like a devil's sick of sin;
If you could hear, at every jolt, the blood
Come gargling from the froth-corrupted lungs,
Obscene as cancer, bitter as the cud
Of vile, incurable sores on innocent tongues,—

what I can't unsee

My friend, you would not tell with such high zest
To children ardent for some desperate glory,
The old Lie: *Dulce et decorum est*
Pro patria mori.

– the saying that is not true

A Truism That's Just Not True

what we were doing	what happened next	how it has haunted me	what I can't unsee	the saying that is <u>not</u> true

Fortis in Arduis

Sitting inside the car in my grandparents' driveway,
cold air sinks in. I clench my sweaty hands,
then reach for my brother, small and quaking.

"It'll be okay," I say.
A lie from the very start.

We watch through the window as my parents rush about
the building at dusk, the silence never breaking.

No news, no news, pressure intensifying,
an ever-growing feeling of doubt
when suddenly a ring. "Any update?"

The car door slams as my feet react before my head.
I run, leaving my brother alone in the car.

Sirens blare distress. I'm hoping and praying,
"Please, don't be dead." For a second, time froze.
Then came the gurney strolling, a hushed moaning.

We watched the ambulance
take our friend Francisco Castillo away.
He died the next day.

My parents tell me "¡se fuerte!"
But no one, no one prepares you for this.
My hope, rationed, little to spare
No one can be prepared: fortis in arduis.

Sarah R. Guerrero
Grade 10

WRITE.

1 Freewrite for 3 minutes (then set aside).

> Think of some scary sounds that would bother you if you heard them at night.

*Nobody starts with a blank page.

READ.

Notice:
- End rhymes
- Internal rhymes
- 6-line stanzas
- trochaic octameter
ˉ˘ ˉ˘ ˉ˘ ˉ˘ ˉ˘ ˉ˘ ˉ˘ ˉ˘

2 Read the poem. Aloud. Slowly. Read it again, and this time everyone should underline parts they find striking. Discuss the parts they notice. Name the craft. Notice the parts.

GET THE STRUCTURE.

3 Reveal the chunked poem. (Students copy the chunks.) Re-read the poem, watching the movement of the structure.

Scary Story

| where I was | a noise I heard | what my mood was | my response to the noise | what appeared | what I asked what it answered × 10 | what is happening now |

WRITE.

4 Invite students to write a poem.
Right now you have
- A page of thoughts
- Examples of craft you like
- A text structure

See what you come up with!
Use any of those, change any, and see what you write in the next minutes.

The Raven
by Edgar Allan Poe

Once upon a midnight dreary, while I pondered,
weak and weary,
Over many a quaint and curious volume of
forgotten lore—
    While I nodded, nearly napping, suddenly
    there came a tapping,
As of some one gently rapping, rapping at my
chamber door.
"'Tis some visitor," I muttered, "tapping at my
chamber door—
        Only this and nothing more."

    Ah, distinctly I remember it was in the bleak
    December;
And each separate dying ember wrought its
ghost upon the floor.
    Eagerly I wished the morrow;—vainly I had
    sought to borrow
    From my books surcease of sorrow—sorrow
    for the lost Lenore—
For the rare and radiant maiden whom the
angels name Lenore—
        Nameless *here* for evermore.

    And the silken, sad, uncertain rustling of
    each purple curtain
Thrilled me—filled me with fantastic terrors
never felt before;
    So that now, to still the beating of my heart,
    I stood repeating
    "'Tis some visitor entreating entrance at my
    chamber door—
Some late visitor entreating entrance at my
chamber door;—
        This it is and nothing more."

    Presently my soul grew stronger; hesitating
    then no longer,
"Sir," said I, "or Madam, truly your forgiveness
I implore;

But the fact is I was napping, and so gently
you came rapping,
And so faintly you came tapping, tapping at
my chamber door,
That I scarce was sure I heard you"—here I
opened wide the door;—
        Darkness there and nothing more.

Deep into that darkness peering, long I
stood there wondering, fearing,
Doubting, dreaming dreams no mortal ever
dared to dream before;
    But the silence was unbroken, and the
    stillness gave no token,
    And the only word there spoken was the
    whispered word, "Lenore?"
This I whispered, and an echo murmured back
the word, "Lenore!"—
        Merely this and nothing more.

    Back into the chamber turning, all my soul
    within me burning,
Soon again I heard a tapping somewhat louder
than before.
    "Surely," said I, "surely that is something at
    my window lattice;
    Let me see, then, what thereat is, and this
    mystery explore—
Let my heart be still a moment and this
mystery explore;—
        'Tis the wind and nothing more!"

Open here I flung the shutter, when, with
many a flirt and flutter,
In there stepped a stately Raven of the saintly
days of yore;
    Not the least obeisance made he; not a
    minute stopped or stayed he;
    But, with mien of lord or lady, perched
    above my chamber door—

(Continued)

(Continued)

Perched upon a bust of Pallas just above my
    chamber door—
        Perched, and sat, and nothing more.

Then this ebony bird beguiling my sad fancy
    into smiling,
By the grave and stern decorum of the
    countenance it wore,
"Though thy crest be shorn and shaven, thou,"
    I said, "art sure no craven,
Ghastly grim and ancient Raven wandering
    from the Nightly shore—
Tell me what thy lordly name is on the Night's
    Plutonian shore!"
        Quoth the Raven "Nevermore."

    Much I marvelled this ungainly fowl to hear
discourse so plainly,
Though its answer little meaning—little
    relevancy bore;
    For we cannot help agreeing that no living
    human being
    Ever yet was blessed with seeing bird above
    his chamber door—
Bird or beast upon the sculptured bust above
    his chamber door,
        With such name as "Nevermore."

    But the Raven, sitting lonely on the placid
bust, spoke only
That one word, as if his soul in that one word
    he did outpour.
    Nothing farther then he uttered—not a
    feather then he fluttered—
    Till I scarcely more than muttered "Other
    friends have flown before—
On the morrow *he* will leave me, as my Hopes
    have flown before."
        Then the bird said "Nevermore."

    Startled at the stillness broken by reply so
aptly spoken,
"Doubtless," said I, "what it utters is its only
    stock and store

Caught from some unhappy master whom
unmerciful Disaster
Followed fast and followed faster till his
songs one burden bore—
Till the dirges of his Hope that melancholy
    burden bore
        Of 'Never—nevermore'."

But the Raven still beguiling all my fancy
    into smiling,
Straight I wheeled a cushioned seat in front of
    bird, and bust and door;
    Then, upon the velvet sinking, I betook
    myself to linking
    Fancy unto fancy, thinking what this
    ominous bird of yore—
What this grim, ungainly, ghastly, gaunt, and
    ominous bird of yore
        Meant in croaking "Nevermore."

This I sat engaged in guessing, but no
    syllable expressing
To the fowl whose fiery eyes now burned into
    my bosom's core;
    This and more I sat divining, with my head at
    ease reclining
    On the cushion's velvet lining that the lamp-
    light gloated o'er,
But whose velvet-violet lining with the lamp-
    light gloating o'er,
        She shall press, ah, nevermore!

Then, methought, the air grew denser,
    perfumed from an unseen censer
Swung by Seraphim whose foot-falls tinkled
    on the tufted floor.
    "Wretch," I cried, "thy God hath lent thee—
    by these angels he hath sent thee
    Respite—respite and nepenthe from thy
    memories of Lenore;
Quaff, oh quaff this kind nepenthe and forget
    this lost Lenore!"
        Quoth the Raven "Nevermore."

"Prophet!" said I, "thing of evil!—prophet still, if bird or devil!—
Whether Tempter sent, or whether tempest tossed thee here ashore,
Desolate yet all undaunted, on this desert land enchanted—
On this home by Horror haunted—tell me truly, I implore—
Is there—*is* there balm in Gilead?—tell me—tell me, I implore!"
Quoth the Raven "Nevermore."

"Prophet!" said I, "thing of evil!—prophet still, if bird or devil!
By that Heaven that bends above us—by that God we both adore—
Tell this soul with sorrow laden if, within the distant Aidenn,
It shall clasp a sainted maiden whom the angels name Lenore—
Clasp a rare and radiant maiden whom the angels name Lenore."
Quoth the Raven "Nevermore."

"Be that word our sign of parting, bird or fiend!" I shrieked, upstarting—
"Get thee back into the tempest and the Night's Plutonian shore!
Leave no black plume as a token of that lie thy soul hath spoken!
Leave my loneliness unbroken!—quit the bust above my door!
Take thy beak from out my heart, and take thy form from off my door!"
Quoth the Raven "Nevermore."

And the Raven, never flitting, still is sitting, *still* is sitting
On the pallid bust of Pallas just above my chamber door;
And his eyes have all the seeming of a demon's that is dreaming,
And the lamp-light o'er him streaming throws his shadow on the floor;
And my soul from out that shadow that lies floating on the floor
Shall be lifted—nevermore!

Source: Edgar Allan Poe, "The Raven," *The Evening Mirror*, 1845.

The Raven
by Edgar Allan Poe

Once upon a midnight dreary, while I
  pondered, weak and weary,
Over many a quaint and curious volume of
  forgotten lore—
While I nodded, nearly napping, suddenly
  there came a tapping,
As of some one gently rapping, rapping at my
  chamber door.
"'Tis some visitor," I muttered, "tapping at my
  chamber door—
    Only this and nothing more."

[handwritten: where I was]
[handwritten: a noise]

Ah, distinctly I remember it was in the bleak
  December;
And each separate dying ember wrought its
  ghost upon the floor.
Eagerly I wished the morrow;—vainly I had
  sought to borrow
From my books surcease of sorrow—sorrow
  for the lost Lenore—
For the rare and radiant maiden whom the
  angels name Lenore—
    Nameless *here* for evermore.

[handwritten: my mood]

And the silken, sad, uncertain rustling of
  each purple curtain
Thrilled me—filled me with fantastic terrors
  never felt before;
So that now, to still the beating of my heart,
  I stood repeating
"'Tis some visitor entreating entrance at my
  chamber door—
Some late visitor entreating entrance at my
  chamber door;—
    This it is and nothing more."

[handwritten: my response to the noise]

Presently my soul grew stronger; hesitating
  then no longer,
"Sir," said I, "or Madam, truly your forgiveness
  I implore;

But the fact is I was napping, and so gently
  you came rapping,
And so faintly you came tapping, tapping at
  my chamber door,
That I scarce was sure I heard you"—here I
  opened wide the door;—
    Darkness there and nothing more.

Deep into that darkness peering, long I
  stood there wondering, fearing,
Doubting, dreaming dreams no mortal ever
  dared to dream before;
But the silence was unbroken, and the
  stillness gave no token,
And the only word there spoken was the
  whispered word, "Lenore?"
This I whispered, and an echo murmured back
  the word, "Lenore!"—
    Merely this and nothing more.

Back into the chamber turning, all my soul
  within me burning,
Soon again I heard a tapping somewhat louder
  than before.
"Surely," said I, "surely that is something at
  my window lattice;
  Let me see, then, what thereat is, and this
  mystery explore—
Let my heart be still a moment and this
  mystery explore;—
    'Tis the wind and nothing more!"

Open here I flung the shutter, when, with
  many a flirt and flutter,
In there stepped a stately Raven of the saintly
  days of yore;
Not the least obeisance made he; not a
  minute stopped or stayed he;
But, with mien of lord or lady, perched
  above my chamber door—

[handwritten: what appeared]

Perched upon a bust of Pallas just above my chamber door—
    Perched, and sat, and nothing more.

Then this ebony bird beguiling my sad fancy into smiling,
By the grave and stern decorum of the countenance it wore,
"Though thy crest be shorn and shaven, thou," I said, "art sure no craven,
Ghastly grim and ancient Raven wandering from the Nightly shore—
Tell me what thy lordly name is on the Night's Plutonian shore!"
    Quoth the Raven "Nevermore."

[handwritten: what I asked]
[handwritten: what it answered]

Much I marvelled this ungainly fowl to hear discourse so plainly,
Though its answer little meaning—little relevancy bore;
For we cannot help agreeing that no living human being
Ever yet was blessed with seeing bird above his chamber door—
Bird or beast upon the sculptured bust above his chamber door,
    With such name as "Nevermore."

But the Raven, sitting lonely on the placid bust, spoke only
That one word, as if his soul in that one word he did outpour.
Nothing farther then he uttered—not a feather then he fluttered—
Till I scarcely more than muttered "Other friends have flown before—
On the morrow *he* will leave me, as my Hopes have flown before."
    Then the bird said "Nevermore."

[handwritten: what I said]
[handwritten: what it answered]

Startled at the stillness broken by reply so aptly spoken,
"Doubtless," said I, "what it utters is its only stock and store

[handwritten: What I said]

Caught from some unhappy master whom unmerciful Disaster
Followed fast and followed faster till his songs one burden bore—
Till the dirges of his Hope that melancholy burden bore
    Of 'Never—nevermore'."

[handwritten: What it answered]

But the Raven still beguiling all my fancy into smiling,
Straight I wheeled a cushioned seat in front of bird, and bust and door;
Then, upon the velvet sinking, I betook myself to linking
Fancy unto fancy, thinking what this ominous bird of yore—
What this grim, ungainly, ghastly, gaunt, and ominous bird of yore
    Meant in croaking "Nevermore."

[handwritten: what I wondered about this]

This I sat engaged in guessing, but no syllable expressing
To the fowl whose fiery eyes now burned into my bosom's core;
This and more I sat divining, with my head at ease reclining
On the cushion's velvet lining that the lamp-light gloated o'er,
But whose velvet-violet lining with the lamp-light gloating o'er,
    She shall press, ah, nevermore!

[handwritten: what I considered]

Then, methought, the air grew denser, perfumed from an unseen censer
Swung by Seraphim whose foot-falls tinkled on the tufted floor.
"Wretch," I cried, "thy God hath lent thee—by these angels he hath sent thee
Respite—respite and nepenthe from thy memories of Lenore;
Quaff, oh quaff this kind nepenthe and forget this lost Lenore!"
    Quoth the Raven "Nevermore."

[handwritten: what I said]
[handwritten: what it answered]

(Continued)

(Continued)

"Prophet!" said I, "thing of evil!—prophet still, if bird or devil!—
Whether Tempter sent, or whether tempest tossed thee here ashore,
Desolate yet all undaunted, on this desert land enchanted—
On this home by Horror haunted—tell me truly, I implore—
Is there—*is* there balm in Gilead?—tell me—tell me, I implore!"
Quoth the Raven "Nevermore."

What I asked

what it answered

"Prophet!" said I, "thing of evil!—prophet still, if bird or devil!
By that Heaven that bends above us—by that God we both adore—
Tell this soul with sorrow laden if, within the distant Aidenn,
It shall clasp a sainted maiden whom the angels name Lenore—
Clasp a rare and radiant maiden whom the angels name Lenore."
Quoth the Raven "Nevermore."

What I said

What it answered

"Be that word our sign of parting, bird or fiend!" I shrieked, upstarting—
"Get thee back into the tempest and the Night's Plutonian shore!
Leave no black plume as a token of that lie thy soul hath spoken!
Leave my loneliness unbroken!—quit the bust above my door!
Take thy beak from out my heart, and take thy form from off my door!"
Quoth the Raven "Nevermore."

What I yelled

What it answered

And the Raven, never flitting, still is sitting, *still* is sitting
On the pallid bust of Pallas just above my chamber door;
And his eyes have all the seeming of a demon's that is dreaming,
And the lamp-light o'er him streaming throws his shadow on the floor;
And my soul from out that shadow that lies floating on the floor
Shall be lifted—nevermore!

What is happening now

Scary Story

where I was	a noise I heard	what my mood was	my response to the noise	what appeared	what I asked / what it answered × 10	what is happening now

The Skull in the Gap

On one very dark and stormy night
I was in my room without a light
trying in vain to rest from the trials of day.
Being tired, I pulled my covers over my head
waiting for my wakefulness to go away,
ignoring my thoughts of tomorrow with dread.

Quite suddenly, I was startled by a wretched noise
a gasp-inducing sound of creaking metal alloys
from my white closet door that cannot close,
leaving a wide slanted gap between itself and wall.
The black gap juxtaposed with the white wall and door
transfixed me by some unknown power to watch it more.
I stared at that gap whose darkness had me in its throes
for how long I don't even know.

I grew irritated that this noise upset my mood so much.
I rose from bed to close the door to end this caliginous gap.
Then, I slunkered to bed to rest for the morrow.
When all of a sudden the noise again my ears did clutch
as I turned to see the gap was back to ruin my nap.
At this point, all I felt was a mixture of annoyance and sorrow.

Not wanting to get up again, I turned over to sleep.
I hoped that in my dreams, over this reality I could leap.
I dreamt of workless days and tireless nights
and soared from lows to unlimited heights.

After a while, I woke into a half-sleep, half-awake trance,
my perception of reality still stuck in a chaotic dance.
Uncomfortable, I attempted to turn over onto my other side
and caught a glimpse of a thing in the gap that made my blood run cold.
There, there was a sinister skull whose surface had long been ossified
in which long crooked teeth pointed in every direction, bold.
I screamed and leapt from my bed, out of my room, and into the hall.

(Continued)

(Continued)

I felt that wretched skull follow me deeper into my dark voided house.
I ran into the front door and having nowhere to go I faced it at last.
Its cranium was white as marble, its sockets each as big as a mouse,
its braincase was a cave, and its open mouth was vast.

I sat on the floor against the front door staring at this floating skull
then mustered the courage I needed to speak to this foul thing.
I sneered: "What are you?"
It boomed to me: **"What I am I am, you cannot construe."**
Confused by this answer I slowly stood upright
to let this monster know that I was not afraid.
I asked of it: "Why are you here?"
It answered: **"Why are YOU here?"**

I realized at once what must be going on.
That this was all a dream that, at sunrise, would soon be gone.
I mocked the skull: "Do you want some paste to make your teeth gleam!?"
It replied in a monotone voice **"This is no dream."**
I realized it was right and that this was a vision,
a foreboding, ominous vision where reality and fiction have a collision.
"WHAT DO YOU WANT FROM ME?" I screamed in the night.
"To give you a fright that is my certain right!"

This horrid creature from across the rivers Lethe, Acheron, and Styx
raced toward my arm and with its teeth bit and gripped.
"You abomination of nature, you falsehood of sense,
for this injury I shall recompense!"
I threw it off but it hovered up again
right in front of me as far as I could ascertain.
**"Do not think that you have the upper score!
I shall haunt you forevermore!"**

"Back to the Phlegethon or Cocytus where you belong
You foul perversion of nature's sweet song!"
**"I will never leave you that is for sure
for the opportunity to torture you I will never abjure!"**
"Soon you'll be gone for the daylight will destroy you
and then I will rejoice in the morning sky of blue."
**"You forget that this is MY domain, this IS the night
where darkness smothers all remaining light!"**

"You shall not win for the die is cast!
Stick around and you'll be in for a blast"
At the fanged skull I threw my lantern,
the dancing fires lit the hallway with their pattern.
The skull was on fire and fell with an intense glare
its every crevice consumed by the now dying flare.

The skull arose still on fire and burnt black in some places
though, it remained mostly white the fire made it visible in small traces.
"Can't anything destroy you?" I said in exasperation.
"Nothing less than a bright burning explosion."
The skull lurched at me again with its mouth wide open
I readied myself and stabbed it with a pen.
"Now your evil has met its end."
"I will be back faster than you can comprehend."

The skull rushed through the hallway into my room
I followed close behind to ensure its doom.
I tried to grab it, but it disappeared through the gap.
I opened the closet to look for this calcium foe.
The closet was empty except for my favorite cap.
The sun came up and my room filled with light and warmth.
The night was dead and the day had come forth.
The skull was now gone and in its place came tomorrow.

Steven Spill
Grade 10

TEACHING NOTES
for "An Essay on Man" (Excerpt)

WRITE.

1 Freewrite for 3 minutes (then set aside).

> Philosophers think about the world and about humans, and about the mysteries that no one can answer.
>
> What are some questions that you have about life? About people? About good and evil?

*Nobody starts with a blank page.

READ.

> Notice
> - heroic couplets
>   iambic pentameter
>   rhyming couplets
>
> - Volta- the turn
>   in the last
>   2 lines

2 Read the poem. Aloud. Slowly. Read it again, and this time everyone should underline parts they find striking. Discuss the parts they notice. Name the craft. Notice the parts.

GET THE STRUCTURE.

3 Reveal the chunked poem. (Students copy the chunks.) Re-read the poem, watching the movement of the structure.

> My Philosophy
>
> | where weaknesses come from | where good things come from | things we can't understand | one thing I know for sure |

WRITE.

4 Invite students to write a poem. Right now you have
- A page of thoughts
- Examples of craft you like
- A text structure

See what you come up with!
Use any of those, change any, and see what you write in the next minutes.

An Essay on Man (Excerpt)
by Alexander Pope

X.

Cease then, nor order imperfection name:

Our proper bliss depends on what we blame.

Know thy own point: This kind, this due degree

Of blindness, weakness, Heav'n bestows on thee.

Submit.—In this, or any other sphere,

Secure to be as blest as thou canst bear:

Safe in the hand of one disposing pow'r,

Or in the natal, or the mortal hour.

All nature is but art, unknown to thee;

All chance, direction, which thou canst not see;

All discord, harmony, not understood;

All partial evil, universal good:

And, spite of pride, in erring reason's spite,

One truth is clear, Whatever is, is right.

Source: Alexander Pope, "An Essay on Man," 1733.

An Essay on Man (Excerpt)
by Alexander Pope

X.

> Cease then, nor order imperfection name:
>
> Our proper bliss depends on what we blame.
>
> Know thy own point: This kind, this due degree
>
> Of blindness, weakness, Heav'n bestows on thee.

where weaknesses come from

> Submit.—In this, or any other sphere,
>
> Secure to be as blest as thou canst bear:
>
> Safe in the hand of one disposing pow'r,
>
> Or in the natal, or the mortal hour.

Where good things come from

> All nature is but art, unknown to thee;
>
> All chance, direction, which thou canst not see;
>
> All discord, harmony, not understood;
>
> All partial evil, universal good:

things we can't understand

> And, spite of pride, in erring reason's spite,
>
> One truth is clear, Whatever is, is right.

one thing I Know for sure

My Philosophy

| where weaknesses come from | where good things come from | things we can't understand | one thing I Know for sure |

My Philosophy

People think *why have I been cursed*
with rules, laws, and ideas
that cannot be put into words?

But through the lens of a simpler view,
people can see the beauty in front of them.
A flower can invite us to dig deep
and think about what is on our mind.

But, a person's drive to find answers
will only cause the mind to drive into a world
of unanswered questions.

Then a moment of clarity is given to you.
You may think of these moments
as a trick from the brain, or a handshake
from God, but no matter what
the gift is clarity and contentment.

Jonas Hinojosa
Grade 9

WRITE.

1 Freewrite for 3 minutes (then set aside).

think of Something in the news, Something that people disagree about.

Write about that.

*Nobody starts with a blank page.

READ.

Notice:
- dialogue
- use of punctuation
- rhyme

2 Read the poem. Aloud. Slowly. Read it again, and this time everyone should underline parts they find striking. Discuss the parts they notice. Name the craft. Notice the parts.

GET THE STRUCTURE.

3 Reveal the chunked poem. (Students copy the chunks.) Re-read the poem, watching the movement of the structure.

Controversial Current Event

| what's happening | voices of people (both for and against) | what most people say | what I say |

WRITE.

4 Invite students to write a poem. Right now you have
- A page of thoughts
- Examples of craft you like
- A text structure

See what you come up with!
Use any of those, change any, and see what you write in the next minutes.

On the Capture and Imprisonment of Crazy Snake, January, 1900
by Alexander Posey

Down with him! chain him! bind him fast!
   Slam to the iron door and turn the key!
The one true Creek, perhaps the last
   To dare declare, "You have wronged me!"
Defiant, stoical, silent,
   Suffers imprisonment!

Such coarse black hair! such eagle eye!
   Such stately mien!—how arrow-straight!
Such will! such courage to defy
   The powerful makers of his fate!
A traitor, outlaw,—what you will,
   He is the noble red man still.

Condemn him and his kind to shame!
   I bow to him, exalt his name!

Source: Alexander Posey, "On the Capture and Imprisonment of Crazy Snake, January, 1900," *The Poems of Alexander Lawrence Posey*, 1910.

**On the Capture and Imprisonment of Crazy Snake, January, 1900
by Alexander Posey**

Down with him! chain him! bind him fast!
    Slam to the iron door and turn the key!
The one true Creek, perhaps the last
    To dare declare, "You have wronged me!"
Defiant, stoical, silent,
    Suffers imprisonment!

what is happening

Such coarse black hair! such eagle eye!
    Such stately mien!—how arrow-straight!
Such will! such courage to defy
    The powerful makers of his fate!
A traitor, outlaw,—what you will,
    He is the noble red man still.

voices of people (both for and against)

Condemn him and his kind to shame!
I bow to him, exalt his name!

*what most people say
—what I say*

Controversial Current Event

what's happening	voices of people (both for and against)	what most people say	what I say

184

The Alabama Abortion Ban

Cuffed in shackles, kept in the corner
Blood under our fingernails from
Metal machinery bites yielding flesh
In dark rooms.

Remnants of a night not yours to remember
Steadily growing under the hands
Of shadows which signed away fate

Protector of tradition
And
Keeper of morality
This is a duty to be fulfilled
Blessed to you

But all teeth and no touch
I'll rebel to keep what's sacred to me
Organs need emptied
Or I'll do it myself

Destruction in sanctified space
But worthy of rebirth

Jana Jarvis
College Student

Earth

pollution
deforestation
human-driven extinction

contaminated air
glaciers melting
our planet growing hot

some people believe it's all politics

but Lil Dicky
brings together
many voices, singing
to show the way:

... it's like we don't know how to act ...

C'mon everybody, I know
we're not all the same, But we're living
on the same Earth.

most people understand
we need to prevent more damage
from being done

recycle
take shorter showers
unplug

I say, take action

Tristen Taylor
Grade 8

WRITE.

1 Freewrite for 3 minutes (then set aside).

List cool things in nature, things that have been there a long time.

*Nobody starts with a blank page.

READ.

Notice:
- personification
- declarative sentences showing authority
- imperative sentences
- interrogative
- allusions to historical events
- specificity of detail

2 Read the poem. Aloud. Slowly. Read it again, and this time everyone should underline parts they find striking. Discuss the parts they notice. Name the craft. Notice the parts.

GET THE STRUCTURE.

3 Reveal the chunked poem. (Students copy the chunks.) Re-read the poem, watching the movement of the structure.

Nature Personified

| What I saw long ago | What I am and what I do | What else I saw long ago | What I will see in the future |

WRITE.

4 Invite students to write a poem.
Right now you have
- A page of thoughts
- Examples of craft you like
- A text structure

See what you come up with!
Use any of those, change any, and see what you write in the next minutes.

Grass
by Carl Sandburg

Pile the bodies high at Austerlitz and Waterloo.
Shovel them under and let me work—
                I am the grass; I cover all.

And pile them high at Gettysburg
And pile them high at Ypres and Verdun.
Shovel them under and let me work.
Two years, ten years, and passengers ask the conductor:
                What place is this?
                Where are we now?

                I am the grass.
                Let me work.

Source: Carl Sandburg, "Grass," *Cornhuskers,* 1918.

Grass
by Carl Sandburg

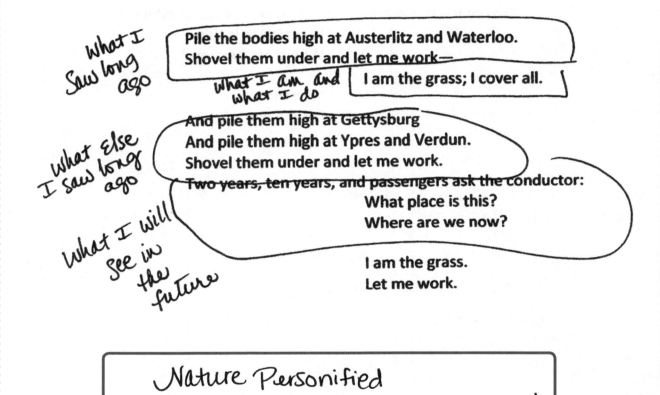

What I Saw long ago

Pile the bodies high at Austerlitz and Waterloo.
Shovel them under and <u>let me work</u>—

What I am and what I do

I am the grass; I cover all.

What Else I saw long ago

And pile them high at Gettysburg
And pile them high at Ypres and Verdun.
Shovel them under and let me work.
Two years, ten years, and passengers ask the conductor:
What place is this?
Where are we now?

what I will See in the future

I am the grass.
Let me work.

Nature Personified

| What I saw long ago | What I am and what I do | what else I saw long ago | what I will see in the future |

Depth of the Deep Blue

Swimming bodies of all kinds.
Creatures of ancient times within the salt of my waves.

I am the deep blue of Earth.
I see all, I am not all seen.

Ships of many have traveled across my surface.
Some have squinted from the glistening blue,
While others tasted the salt in their chains.
Various levels of the ship creates
Different ways of voyaging.

My blue has been vast, deep.
In time to come, will I be gone?
Will I get to see the bottom?
Is there really an end to this depth?
I may see an uncountable amount of skeletons.
Skulls of the salt-water breathers,
Rotten teeth of the voyagers.

I am the blue of this earth.
Let me be the beholder of life and mysteries.

Tae Lennon
Grade 12

WRITE.

1 Freewrite for 3 minutes (then set aside).

Think about "perfect" looks, life. Describe what most people consider to be "perfect."
(2 minutes ↑) (1 minute ↓)
Write about someone meaningful to you (friend or family). Describe your favorite things about them.

*Nobody starts with a blank page.

READ.

Notice:
• Shakespearean Sonnet
(3 quatrains + 1 couplet)
Rhyme Scheme
   ABAB
   CDCD
   EFEF
   GG
Tone created by the comparisons

2 Read the poem. Aloud. Slowly. Read it again, and this time everyone should underline parts they find striking. Discuss the parts they notice. Name the craft. Notice the parts.

GET THE STRUCTURE.

3 Reveal the chunked poem. (Students copy the chunks.) Re-read the poem, watching the movement of the structure.

the Real (Not "Perfect") Person

| "ways my person is not perfect (compared to the "perfect" person) | more ways my person is <u>not</u> perfect | things my person does not do perfectly | yet how I feel about my person |

WRITE.

4 Invite students to write a poem.
Right now you have
• A page of thoughts
• Examples of craft you like
• A text structure

See what you come up with!
Use any of those, change any, and see what you write in the next minutes.

Sonnet 130: My Mistress' Eyes Are Nothing Like the Sun
by William Shakespeare

My mistress' eyes are nothing like the sun;
Coral is far more red than her lips' red;
If snow be white, why then her breasts are dun;
If hairs be wires, black wires grow on her head.
I have seen roses damasked, red and white,
But no such roses see I in her cheeks;
And in some perfumes is there more delight
Than in the breath that from my mistress reeks.
I love to hear her speak, yet well I know
That music hath a far more pleasing sound;
I grant I never saw a goddess go;
My mistress, when she walks, treads on the ground.
   And yet, by heaven, I think my love as rare
   As any she belied with false compare.

Source: William Shakespeare, "Sonnet 130: My Mistress' Eyes Are Nothing Like the Sun," 1609.

**Sonnet 130: My Mistress' Eyes Are
Nothing Like the Sun
by William Shakespeare**

My mistress' eyes are nothing like the sun;
Coral is far more red than her lips' red;
If snow be white, why then her breasts are dun;
If hairs be wires, black wires grow on her head.

ways my person is not perfect

I have seen roses damasked, red and white,
But no such roses see I in her cheeks;
And in some perfumes is there more delight
Than in the breath that from my mistress reeks.

more ways

I love to hear her speak, yet well I know
That music hath a far more pleasing sound;
I grant I never saw a goddess go;
My mistress, when she walks, treads on the ground.

things my person does not do perfectly

And yet, by heaven, I think my love as rare
As any she belied with false compare.

how I feel about my person

the Real (Not "Perfect") Person

| *ways my person is not perfect (compared to the "perfect" person)* | *more ways my person is not perfect* | *things my person does not do perfectly* | *yet how I feel about my person* |

Sonnet

The girl I carry fondness for
Is not a pretty girl at all.
Her manners are as poor
as the oak tree's colors in fall.
She's indecisive. Insecure.
And though she acts naïve she
uses her emotions as a lure
and cries until I run back
to her tangled hair and twisted lies.
She screeches that she loves me
and needs me to survive.
Her talons claw into my chest
and drag me back to her again.
Even though I know it'll pain me
I want to be her friend.

Alex Calvio
Grade 12

Sonnet

My teacher's classroom is dark as night.
She may not be the absolute best.
When you make a mistake, she may put up a fight.
Sometimes it's too much, she may need to rest.
Her short temper can give you a fright.
She makes mistakes that are obvious.
Even though her room isn't that bright
you want to know where she is.
She doesn't give us visible help,
her mood can change like a weather forecast.
When she's anxious, she'll let out a big yelp.
Her knowledge about other subjects isn't vast,
yet she does everything to help with our grade.
She's one of the reasons we all stayed.

Malachi Suarez
Grade 9

Perfection, He Is Not

His eyes do not glimmer like a star.
If smiles could be bright, then his would be dim.
In large crowds, he avoids and stays clear,
anxiety devouring each inch of him.

The smell of rotting fruit on a spring day
is better than hugging him.
Yes, he lacks the ability to be happy,
he's not pleasant, and his clothes are a mess.

Expressing emotion, he lost that skill.
He never really speaks in a sweet tone.
But I never knew how lucky I was until
I lost him, when he used to be my own.

He'll always be there no matter what
I will always remember him in my gut.

Kaidlyn Allison
Grade 7

Island

This island is too hot for me.
Killer whales try to eat us,
and there's the salty smell of the salty sea.
Sand is everywhere.
Something's trying to bite my legs,
something I cannot bear.
Then there's the smell of rotten eggs,
volcanoes erupting rocks shore to shore,
there's nothing to do, it's not fun,
but there's something fun about this place
that's new. That thing is you.

Rosi Jones
Grade 7

WRITE.

1 Freewrite for 3 minutes (then set aside).

Make a list of things you've seen that were broken.

Describe one you remember most clearly.

*Nobody starts with a blank page.

READ.

Notice:
- frame device
- Petrarchan sonnet form
- iambic pentameter
- irony
- ambiguity (whose hand mocked?)

2 Read the poem. Aloud. Slowly. Read it again, and this time everyone should underline parts they find striking. Discuss the parts they notice. Name the craft. Notice the parts.

GET THE STRUCTURE.

3 Reveal the chunked poem. (Students copy the chunks.) Re-read the poem, watching the movement of the structure.

Retelling a Story (by looking at Shards)

| Who had this experience | one broken part I saw | another part and what I could tell about it | another part I saw | what was around it |

WRITE.

4 Invite students to write a poem.
Right now you have
- A page of thoughts
- Examples of craft you like
- A text structure

See what you come up with!
Use any of those, change any, and see what you write in the next minutes.

Ozymandias
by Percy Bysshe Shelley

I met a traveller from an antique land,
Who said—"Two vast and trunkless legs of stone
Stand in the desert. . . . Near them, on the sand,
Half sunk a shattered visage lies, whose frown,
And wrinkled lip, and sneer of cold command,
Tell that its sculptor well those passions read
Which yet survive, stamped on these lifeless things,
The hand that mocked them, and the heart that fed;
And on the pedestal, these words appear:
My name is Ozymandias, King of Kings;
Look on my Works, ye Mighty, and despair!
Nothing beside remains. Round the decay
Of that colossal Wreck, boundless and bare
The lone and level sands stretch far away."

Source: Percy Bysshe Shelley, "Ozymandias," *The Examiner*, 1818.

Ozymandias
by Percy Bysshe Shelley

I met a traveller from an antique land, *Who had this experience*

Who said—"Two vast and trunkless legs of stone *one broken part I saw*

Stand in the desert. . .. Near them, on the sand,

Half sunk a shattered visage lies, whose frown, *another part and what I could tell about it*

And wrinkled lip, and sneer of cold command,

Tell that its sculptor well those passions read

Which yet survive, stamped on these lifeless things,

The hand that mocked them, and the heart that fed;

And on the pedestal, these words appear: *another part I saw*

My name is Ozymandias, King of Kings;

Look on my Works, ye Mighty, and despair!

Nothing beside remains. Round the decay

Of that colossal Wreck, boundless and bare *what was around it*

The lone and level sands stretch far away."

Retelling a Story (by Looking at Shards)

| who had this experience | one broken part I saw | another part and what I could tell about it | another part I saw | what was around it |

Lightbulb in the Green

Shattered glass on the green ground.
Clear shards cut the living.
Leaves bend to the sharp touch.
Sun shines upon the pieces while
The leaves weep.

Fragments of the glass surround.
None make a sound,
But rather show their presence through
The sunlight's spotlight.
Sun rays glisten off
Of every sliver.

Joaquin Walker
Grade 12

READ.

Notice:
• Poetic form
  VILLANELLE
  (Pattern of repetition
  in lines 1 and 3
  throughout the poem)
  + Color-coding reveals
  the pattern.

• Iambic pentameter
• Urgent argument

WRITE.

1 Freewrite for 3 minutes (then set aside).

Think of a time someone was handling something all wrong. Describe that time. What do you think they should have done?

*Nobody starts with a blank page.

2 Read the poem. Aloud. Slowly.
Read it again, and this time everyone should underline parts they find striking. Discuss the parts they notice. Name the craft. Notice the parts.

GET THE STRUCTURE.

3 Reveal the chunked poem. (Students copy the chunks.) Re-read the poem, watching the movement of the structure.

(Villanelle) Advice

| what people should do in this situation | one group and how they handle it correctly | another group and how they handle it correctly | another group and how they handle it correctly | my advice to the person doing the wrong thing |

WRITE.

4 Invite students to write a poem.
Right now you have
  • A page of thoughts
  • Examples of craft you like
  • A text structure

See what you come up with!
Use any of those, change any, and see what you write in the next minutes.

Do Not Go Gentle Into That Good Night
by Dylan Thomas

Do not go gentle into that good night,
Old age should burn and rave at close of day;
Rage, rage against the dying of the light.

Though wise men at their end know dark is right,
Because their words had forked no lightning they
Do not go gentle into that good night.

Good men, the last wave by, crying how bright
Their frail deeds might have danced in a green bay,
Rage, rage against the dying of the light.

Wild men who caught and sang the sun in flight,
And learn, too late, they grieved it on its way,
Do not go gentle into that good night.

Grave men, near death, who see with blinding sight
Blind eyes could blaze like meteors and be gay,
Rage, rage against the dying of the light.

And you, my father, there on the sad height,
Curse, bless, me now with your fierce tears, I pray.
Do not go gentle into that good night.
Rage, rage against the dying of the light.

TEXT STRUCTURE
From "Do Not Go Gentle Into That Good Night"

Do Not Go Gentle Into That Good Night
by Dylan Thomas

Do not go gentle into that good night,
Old age should burn and rave at close of day;
Rage, rage against the dying of the light.

what people should do in this situation

Though wise men at their end know dark is right,
Because their words had forked no lightning they
Do not go gentle into that good night.

one group and how they handle it correctly

Good men, the last wave by, crying how bright
Their frail deeds might have danced in a green bay,
Rage, rage against the dying of the light.

another group and how they handle it correctly

Wild men who caught and sang the sun in flight,
And learn, too late, they grieved it on its way,
Do not go gentle into that good night.

another group and how they handle it correctly

Grave men, near death, who see with blinding sight
Blind eyes could blaze like meteors and be gay,
Rage, rage against the dying of the light.

another group and how they handle it correctly

And you, my father, there on the sad height,
Curse, bless, me now with your fierce tears, I pray.
Do not go gentle into that good night.
Rage, rage against the dying of the light

my advice (urging)

(Villanelle) Advice

what people should do in this situation	one group and how they handle it correctly	another group and how they handle it correctly	another group and how they handle it correctly	my advice to the person doing the wrong thing

Flames Won't End the Pain

Do not mend your wounds with raging fire
the relief is only brief, and burns you away
pain, pain is not life's entire

Healers blaze with love that inspires
they treat scars with care, they
do not mend wounds with raging fire

Some friends have lots of true desire
to guide you in a burning way
pain, pain is not life's entire

Preachers give praise when others are in dire
need of healing and love and then say:
Do not mend wound with raging fire

The voice inside might say: "Jump off the wire
into the gorge" where hope cannot stay
pain, pain is not life's entire

Death is not the way to soar higher
hold on, I tell you the end's not today
do not mend wounds with raging fire
pain, pain is not life's entire

Abigail Henning
Grade 7

WRITE.

1 Freewrite for 3 minutes (then set aside).

Did you ever pick up something in nature and keep it, like a little souvenir... like a flower or a rock? Think back and write about that.

*Nobody starts with a blank page.

READ.

Notice:
- inverted syntax (strange order of words in the second line)
- interesting parenthetical part

2 Read the poem. Aloud. Slowly. Read it again, and this time everyone should underline parts they find striking. Discuss the parts they notice. Name the craft. Notice the parts.

GET THE STRUCTURE.

3 Reveal the chunked poem. (Students copy the chunks.) Re-read the poem, watching the movement of the structure.

Metaphor of Myself

| a description of what I saw | how it's like me | how it's not like me | what I kept and why | What I think (about me) when I look at it |

WRITE.

4 Invite students to write a poem. Right now you have
- A page of thoughts
- Examples of craft you like
- A text structure

See what you come up with!
Use any of those, change any, and see what you write in the next minutes.

I Saw in Louisiana a Live-Oak Growing
by Walt Whitman

I saw in Louisiana a live-oak growing,
All alone stood it and the moss hung down from the branches,
Without any companion it grew there uttering joyous leaves of dark green,
And its look, rude, unbending, lusty, made me think of myself,
But I wonder'd how it could utter joyous leaves standing alone there without its
    friend near, for I knew I could not,
And I broke off a twig with a certain number of leaves upon it, and twined around
    it a little moss,
And brought it away, and I have placed it in sight in my room,
It is not needed to remind me as of my own dear friends,
(For I believe lately I think of little else than of them,)
Yet it remains to me a curious token, it makes me think of manly love;
For all that, and though the live-oak glistens there in Louisiana solitary in a wide flat
    space,
Uttering joyous leaves all its life without a friend a lover near,
I know very well I could not.

Source: Walt Whitman, "I Saw in Louisiana a Live-Oak Growing," *Leaves of Grass,* 1892.

I Saw in Louisiana a Live-Oak Growing
by Walt Whitman

I saw in Louisiana a live-oak growing,
All alone stood it and the moss hung down from the branches,
Without any companion it grew there uttering joyous leaves of dark green, — *What I Saw*
And its look, rude, unbending, lusty, made me think of myself, ← *how it's like me*
But I wonder'd how it could utter joyous leaves standing alone there without its
    friend near, for I knew I could not, — *not like me*
And I broke off a twig with a certain number of leaves upon it, and twined around it
    a little moss,
And brought it away, and I have placed it in sight in my room,
It is not needed to remind me as of my own dear friends,
(For I believe lately I think of little else than of them,)
Yet it remains to me a curious token, it makes me think of manly love; — *What I Kept and WHY*
For all that, and though the live-oak glistens there in Louisiana solitary in a wide flat
    space,
Uttering joyous leaves all its life without a friend a lover near,
I know very well I could not.

what I think (about me)

Metaphor of Myself

a description of what I saw	how its like me	how its **not** like me	what I Kept and why	What I think (about me) when I look at it

Bullet

One morning I found something and had no doubt
that what I found was a gold cylinder with a red glow, a glow
so colorful, so vibrant, so rich almost like it was trying to possess me

almost calling to me, the red glow so tempting
that I started to feel red inside
almost angry at the world for no reason.

But the more I looked at the bullet, the more it became haunting.
I could hear cries and screams that came from it.
I became more aware, more aware of this world
and how cruel it can be.

Five minutes of staring at this, this creator
of mass destruction, I picked it up carefully
trying not to startle it
in fear that it might awake and attack.

I picked it up so no one will ever look at a bullet
and be tempted like I almost was.

After that day, I thought of all the other things
that would bring terror and fear.

Josiah Moreno
Grade 6

READ.

Notice:
- use of capitals
- Simile, extended
- personification
- imagery
- motion verbs

WRITE.

1 Freewrite for 3 minutes (then set aside).

Think of something you saw that was so hard to describe-- it left an impression (like stars in a dark sky) so unusual, so extra-ordinary, you can still see it in your mind's eye.

*Nobody starts with a blank page.

2 Read the poem. Aloud. Slowly. Read it again, and this time everyone should underline parts they find striking. Discuss the parts they notice. Name the craft. Notice the parts.

GET THE STRUCTURE.

3 Reveal the chunked poem. (Students copy the chunks.) Re-read the poem, watching the movement of the structure.

A Staggering Thing I Saw

| what I was doing | what Staggering thing I saw | how it made me feel right then | how that memory helps/affects me now |

WRITE.

4 Invite students to write a poem. Right now you have
- A page of thoughts
- Examples of craft you like
- A text structure

See what you come up with!
Use any of those, change any, and see what you write in the next minutes.

I Wandered Lonely as a Cloud
by William Wordsworth

I wandered lonely as a Cloud
That floats on high o'er Vales and Hills,
When all at once I saw a crowd,
A host, of golden Daffodils;
Beside the Lake, beneath the trees,
Fluttering and dancing in the breeze.

Continuous as the stars that shine
And twinkle on the Milky Way,
They stretched in never-ending line
Along the margin of a bay:
Ten thousand saw I at a glance,
Tossing their heads in sprightly dance.

The waves beside them danced; but they
Out-did the sparkling waves in glee:
A Poet could not but be gay,
In such a jocund company:
I gazed—and gazed—but little thought
What wealth the show to me had brought:

For oft, when on my couch I lie
In vacant or in pensive mood,
They flash upon that inward eye
Which is the bliss of solitude;
And then my heart with pleasure fills,
And dances with the Daffodils.

Source: William Wordsworth, "I Wandered Lonely as a Cloud," *Poems, in Two Volumes,* 1807.

I Wandered Lonely as a Cloud
by William Wordsworth

I wandered lonely as a Cloud
That floats on high o'er Vales and Hills, ⟩ *what I was doing*

When all at once I saw a crowd,
A host, of golden Daffodils;
Beside the Lake, beneath the trees,
Fluttering and dancing in the breeze.

Continuous as the stars that shine
And twinkle on the Milky Way, *what I saw*
They stretched in never-ending line
Along the margin of a bay:
Ten thousand saw I at a glance,
Tossing their heads in sprightly dance.

The waves beside them danced; but they
Out-did the sparkling waves in glee:
A Poet could not but be gay, *how it made me feel*
In such a jocund company:

I gazed—and gazed—but little thought
What wealth the show to me had brought:

For oft, when on my couch I lie *how that*
In vacant or in pensive mood, *memory*
They flash upon that inward eye *helps me*
Which is the bliss of solitude; *now*
And then my heart with pleasure fills,
And dances with the Daffodils.

A Staggering Thing I Saw

| What I was doing | What Staggering thing I saw | how it made me feel right then | how that memory helps/affects me now |

Wonderful Day

The band plays the interlude
as I sit there, wonder on my face,
when a familiar tune starts to play.
The sea of fans scream,
an avalanche of noise and emotion.

A rainbow of hearts flashes through the crowd
as people pull out Pride flags,
smiles miles wide.
The chorus starts
and the crowd grows louder and louder,
singing our hearts out to the song.

Rainbows flood out of the crowd,
and I'm filled with glee.
This is the only place
I ever wanted to be
with people laughing and dancing all around me.

When I look back at it now,
I can't help but smile,
thinking of the world of rainbows and prisms
that were mine for a while.

Aaminah Zeinelabdin
Grade 7

The Lone Pump Jack

Driving early in the morn,
leaving Midland and my love,
I saw in silhouette against the sky—
indigo, pink and orange—
a pump jack dark as coal.

It stood out, stark and black,
and though so many pumps dot the land,
this one is a world all its own,
a thing of beauty, quiet
amid the traffic and the noise.
I wanted to drink it in.

I keep that road hot, driving
through dusk or morning's first light,
thinking not of the boring land,
but of a lone pump jack dark as night.

Lorrie Payne
Educator

Glimpses of the Majestic Theater:
The Atmosphere from Space

I step onto the balcony into a dream-like scene.
The dark lights resemble a cosmic ocean in space.
The still birds and scenes from nature
wrap an illusion of the outdoors around me.
I take a seat. The beauty intoxicates me.
I feel drunk with delight. I am speechless.
I lie back and enjoy a show from the heavens.

Jonas Hinojosa
Grade 9

TEACHING NOTES
for "When You Are Old"

WRITE.

1 Freewrite for 3 minutes (then set aside).

Think about one person you always want to remember you... think of someone close to you. What do you hope they always remember about you?

*Nobody starts with a blank page.

READ.

Notice:
- personification
- direct address
- point of view (written as 3rd person)
- hard rhymes
- rhyme scheme ABBA

2 Read the poem. Aloud. Slowly. Read it again, and this time everyone should underline parts they find striking. Discuss the parts they notice. Name the craft. Notice the parts.

GET THE STRUCTURE.

3 Reveal the chunked poem. (Students copy the chunks.) Re-read the poem, watching the movement of the structure.

Instructions for Remembering

| when you should read this and what you should think about | what good qualities most people know about you | your best quality (that I see) | where you can find me later |

WRITE.

4 Invite students to write a poem. Right now you have
- A page of thoughts
- Examples of craft you like
- A text structure

See what you come up with!
Use any of those, change any, and see what you write in the next minutes.

When You Are Old
by William Butler Yeats

When you are old and grey and full of sleep,
And nodding by the fire, take down this book,
And slowly read, and dream of the soft look
Your eyes had once, and of their shadows deep;

How many loved your moments of glad grace,
And loved your beauty with love false or true,
But one man loved the pilgrim soul in you,
And loved the sorrows of your changing face;

And bending down beside the glowing bars,
Murmur, a little sadly, how Love fled
And paced upon the mountains overhead
And hid his face amid a crowd of stars.

Source: William Butler Yeats, "When You Are Old," *The Rose*, 1893.

When You Are Old
by William Butler Yeats

When you are old and grey and full of sleep,
And nodding by the fire, take down this book,
And slowly read, and dream of the soft look
Your eyes had once, and of their shadows deep;

when you should read this and what you should think about

How many loved your moments of glad grace,
And loved your beauty with love false or true,
But one man loved the pilgrim soul in you,
And loved the sorrows of your changing face;

– what good qualities most people see in you

your best qualities that I see in you

And bending down beside the glowing bars,
Murmur, a little sadly, how Love fled
And paced upon the mountains overhead
And hid his face amid a crowd of stars.

where you can find me later

Instructions for Remembering

when you should read this and what you should think about	what good qualities most people know about you	your best quality (that I see)	where you can find me later

I Keep Remembering

My best friend is moving to Colorado
while I'm staying in Ohio.
I hope he doesn't forget our times,
because we were partners in crime.

I was always the good guy,
the guy who flies high.
He was the kid who made me laugh.
We were two wholes and now we are only halves.

Now I sit alone in my big house
I look in the dark hole and hear a mouse.
I'm here in Ohio, left in my home,
sitting in a recliner chair waiting for the phone.

I think, "Why not sing a song?"
Ring ding dong my friend is gone
come back where you belong.
The phone rang, and it was my friend.
I told him don't worry I'll be your friend to the end.

Jeremiah Small
Grade 7

To My Cousin

When you are going into motherhood
and the kids are frustrating you,
bring back the memory of us as kids
jumping in the pool.

Do not worry. People love you,
the way you strive to have fun.
They get a wave of joy when you pass by
and never want you to leave.

I love you too,
I put my trust in you. Don't let go,
no matter how hard it gets. Cousin,
I know I don't deserve you.

No matter how far apart we live,
I'll always be right there.
You can call me whenever,
and come over any time.

Sarah Vaughn
Grade 7

Appendices

Appendix 1

Complete Collection of 50 Text Structures

Acting On Impulse

- Things I see that make me feel/think/react
- What I wish I could say
- but how the world expects us to react
- Instead, I decide to do/say ___
- the reaction I get

A place (and its Sensory Details)

- What you see, smell, hear in that place
- one thing you learned in that place
- other sensory things that always happen there

What I Give to You

- What I offer you
- what it is like
- What else it is
- what you can do with it
- when you'll need it most

Quirky Behavior

- the quirky thing they do
- Why they do it
- What it makes me wonder
- What they would answer

Memories Unique to You (List/Anaphora)

- one weird thing I remember
- another weird thing I remember
- another weird thing I remember
- ← repeat until you're done

Watching Someone Do Something

- What they are doing as you watch
- What you see when you shift your gaze to the outside
- what new thing you see when you look at the person now
- a question about a change coming in your future

Appendix 1   **215**

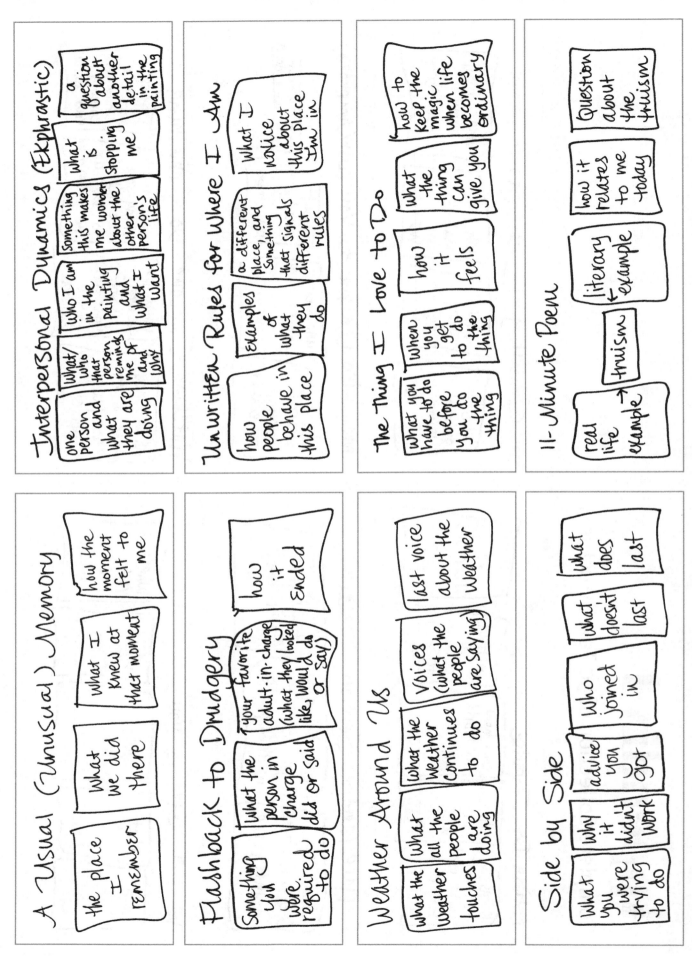

Interpersonal Dynamics (Ekphrastic)

- one person and what they are doing
- What/who that person reminds me of and why
- Who I am in the painting and what I want
- Something this makes me wonder about the other person's life
- what is stopping me
- a question about another detail in the painting

Unwritten Rules for Where I Am

- how people behave in this place
- Examples of what they do
- a different place, and something that signals different rules
- What I notice about this place I'm in

The Thing I Love to Do

- what you have to do before you do the thing
- when you get to do the thing
- how it feels
- what the thing can give you
- how to keep the magic when life becomes ordinary

11-Minute Poem

- real life example → truism ← literary example
- how it relates to me today
- Question about the truism

A Usual (Unusual) Memory

- the place I remember
- What we did there
- what I knew at that moment
- how the moment felt to me

Flashback to Drudgery

- Something you were required to do
- What the person in charge did or said
- your favorite adult-in-charge (what they looked like, would do or say)
- how it ended

Weather Around Us

- what the weather touches
- what all the people are doing
- what the weather continues to do
- Voices (what the people are saying)
- last voice about the weather

Side by Side

- What you were trying to do
- why it didn't work
- advice you got
- Who joined in
- what doesn't last
- what does last

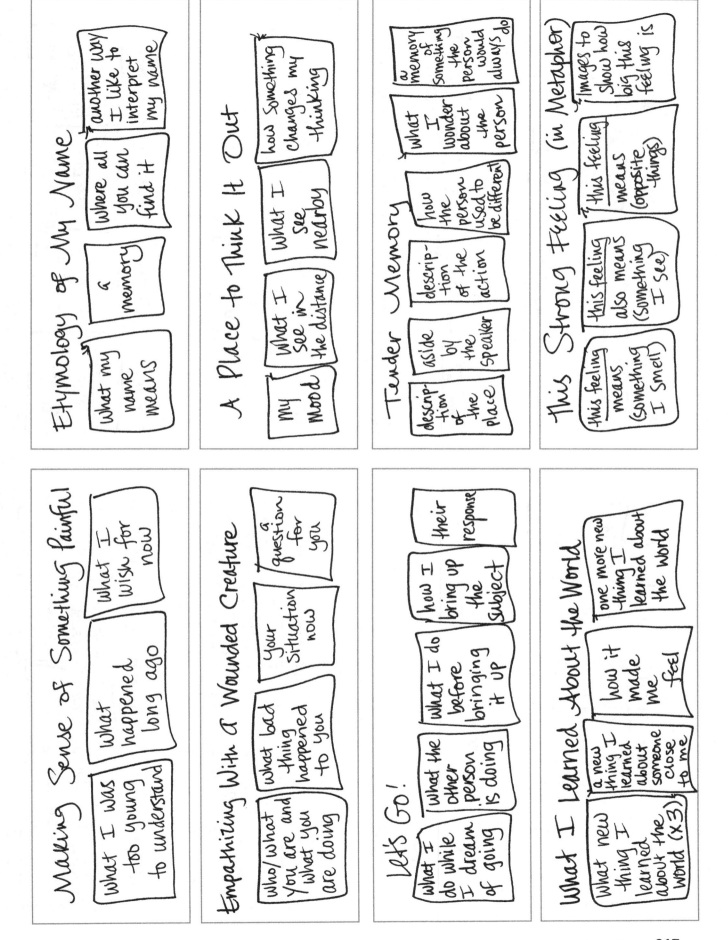

Etymology of My Name

- What my name means
- a memory
- Where all you can find it
- another way I like to interpret my name

A Place to Think It Out

- My Mood
- What I see in the distance
- What I see nearby
- how something changes my thinking

Tender Memory

- description of the place
- aside by the speaker
- description of the action
- how the person used to be different
- What I wonder about the person
- a memory of something the person would always do

This Strong Feeling (in Metaphor)

- this feeling means (something I smell)
- this feeling also means (something I see)
- this feeling means (opposite things)
- images to show how big this feeling is

Making Sense of Something Painful

- What I was too young to understand
- what happened long ago
- What I wish for now

Empathizing With a Wounded Creature

- Who/what you are and what you are doing
- what bad thing happened to you
- Your situation now
- a question for you

Let's Go!

- What I do while I dream of going
- What the other person is doing
- what I do before bringing it up
- how I bring up the subject
- their response

What I Learned About the World

- What new thing I learned about the world (x3)
- a new thing I learned about someone close to me
- how it made me feel
- one more new thing I learned about the world

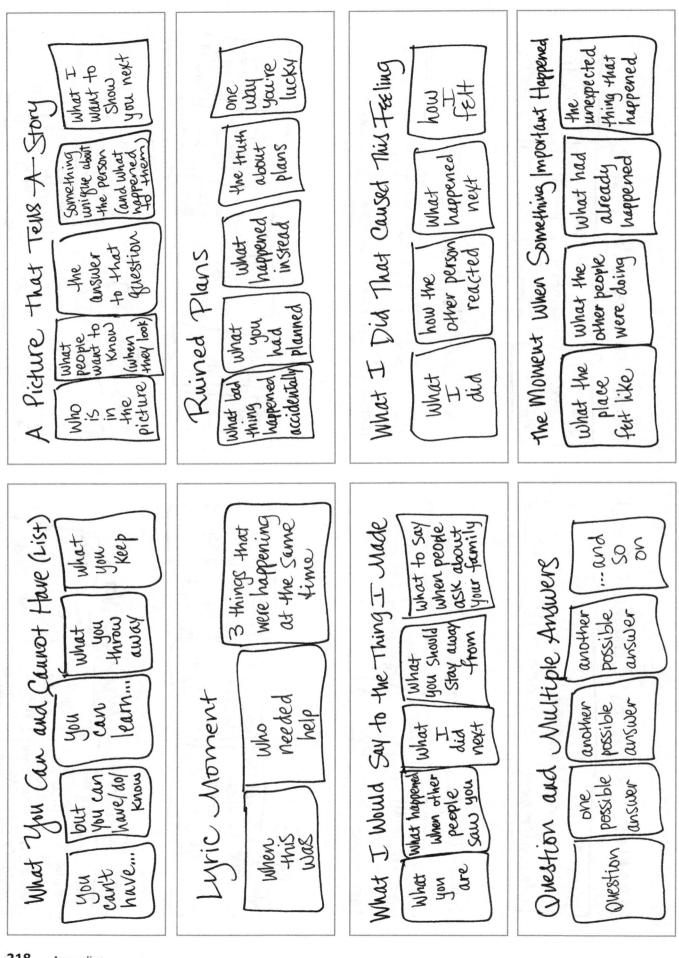

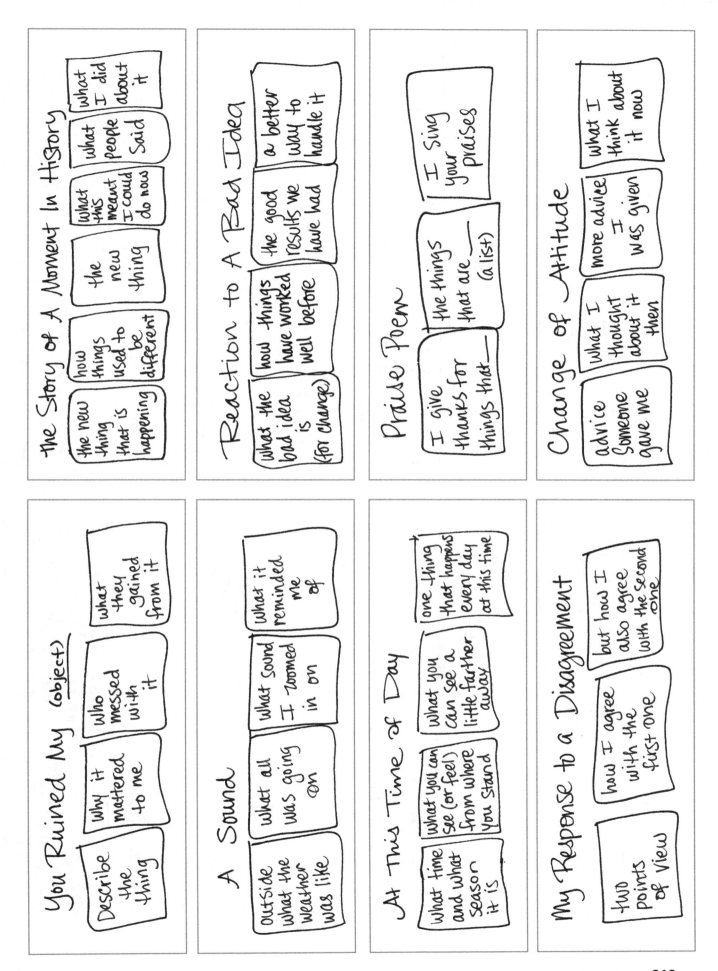

The Story of A Moment In History

the new thing that is happening → how things used to be different → the new thing → what this meant I could do now → what people said → what I did about it

Reaction to A Bad Idea

what the bad idea is (for change) → how things have worked well before → the good results we have had → a better way to handle it

Praise Poem

I give thanks for things that ___ → the things that are ___ (a list) → I sing your praises

Change of Attitude

advice someone gave me → what I thought about it then → more advice I was given → what I think about it now

You Ruined My (object)

Describe the thing → why it mattered to me → who messed with it → what they gained from it

A Sound

Outside what the weather was like → what all was going on → what sound I zoomed in on → what it reminded me of

At This Time of Day

What time and what season it is → what you can see (or feel) from where you stand → what you can see a little farther away → one thing that happens every day at this time

My Response to a Disagreement

two points of view → how I agree with the first one → but how I also agree with the second one

Controversial Current Event

what's happening → Voices of people (both for and against) → what most people say → What I say

Nature Personified

what I saw long ago → what I am and what I do → what else I saw long ago → what I will see in the future

The Real (Not "Perfect") Person

"ways my person is not perfect (compared to the "perfect" person) → more ways my person is NOT perfect → things my person does not do perfectly → Yet how I feel about my person

Retelling a Story (by looking at Shards)

Who had this experience → one broken part I saw → another part and what I could tell about it → another part I saw → what was around it

The Thing That Got Away

describe what you wanted → What happens when you try to get it → then what happens → how it gets away

A Truism That's Just Not True

what we were doing → what happened next → how it has haunted me → what I can't unsee → the saying that is not true

Scary Story

where I was → a noise I heard → what my mood was → my response to the noise → what appeared → what I asked / what it answered ×10 → what is happening now

My Philosophy

where weaknesses come from → where good things come from → things we can't understand → one thing I know for sure

A Staggering Thing I Saw

- What I was doing
- What staggering thing I saw
- how it made me feel right then
- how that memory helps/affects me now

Instructions for Remembering

- when you should read this and what you should think about
- what good qualities most people know about you
- your best quality (that I see)
- where you can find me later

(Villanelle) Advice

- What people should do in this situation
- One group and how they handle it correctly
- another group and how they handle it correctly
- my advice to the person doing the wrong thing

Metaphor of Myself

- a description of what I saw
- how it's like me
- how it's not like me
- what I kept and why
- what I think (about me) when I look at it

Appendix 2

Glossary: Fixed Forms

Petrarchan Sonnet **(Lesson 30)**	The Italian poet Petrarch perfected a sonnet form where 14 lines are divided into two sections—an 8-line stanza (octave) and a 6-line stanza (sestet) written in iambic pentameter. The volta, or turn of thought, occurs between the octave and the sestet—often the octave sets up an argument or a problem and the sestet offers a response to it. The Petrarchan sonnet follows the following rhyme (variable) pattern: *Octave:* abba abba *Sestet:* cdcdcd or cdeede
Shakespearean Sonnet **(Lessons 26, 46)**	The form of a sonnet used by Shakespeare that is 14 lines, consisting of three quatrains and a final couplet written in iambic pentameter. The volta, or the turn of thought or argument, occurs before the final couplet. The Shakespearean sonnet follows the following rhyme pattern: abba cdcd efef gg
Villanelle **(Lesson 47)**	A 19-line French form consisting of five three-line stanzas and a final quatrain. The first and third lines of the first stanza repeat, alternating in the following stanzas. The two repeated lines appear as the final couplet in the poem. The villanelle resists narrative progression and embraces a cyclical movement, teasing out and exploring a concept or idea. The Villanelle follows the following rhyme pattern: aba aba aba aba aba abaa

Appendix 3

Glossary: Meter

Iambic Pentameter	A line of verse consisting of five metrical feet where each is made up of one iamb, which is one unstressed syllable followed by a stressed syllable.
	My MIS | tress' EYS | are NO | thing LIKE | the SUN
	Source: From "Sonnet 130" by William Shakespeare
Hymn Meter	Consists of four lines rhyming abab (or sometimes abcb) where lines one and three are iambic tetrameter, and two and four are iambic trimeter.
	outSIDE | the RAIN | upon | the STREET the SKY | all GRIM | of HUE inSIDE | the MUS | ic PAIN | ful SWEET and YET | i HEARD | but YOU
	as IS | a THRILL | ing VI | olIN so IS | your VOICE | to ME and STILL | aBOVE | the OTH | her STRAINS it SANG | in EC | staCY
	Source: "A Musical" by Paul Lawrence Dunbar
Trochaic Octameter	Consists of eight metrical feet per line where each is made up of a trochee, which is one stressed syllable followed by an unstressed syllable.
	ONCE u | PON a | MIDnight| DREARy | WHILE i | PONdered | WEAK and | WEARy … .
	Source: From "The Raven" by Edgar Allan Poe
Tetrameter	A line of verse consisting of four metrical feet where each is made up of one iamb, which is one unstressed syllable followed by a stressed syllable.
	i SAID | a THOUGHT | less WORD | one DAY a LOVED | one HEARD | and WENT | aWAY
	Source: From "Regret" by Olivia Ward Bush-Banks

Appendix 4

Glossary: Rhyme

Rhymed Couplets (Lessons 25, 27, 29, 42)	Two consecutive lines in a poem that rhyme and complete a thought. And for thy Mother, she alas is POOR, Which caus'd her thus to send thee out of DOOR. *Source:* From "The Author to Her Book" by Anne Bradstreet
Hard Rhyme (Lessons 31, 50)	Rhymes where the stressed syllable are exact sonic matches. It sucked me first, and now sucks THEE, And in this flea our two bloods mingled BE; *Source:* From "The Flea" by John Donne
Slant Rhyme (Lessons 26, 31)	Rhymes where the stressed syllables are *near* sonic matches. Oh stay, there lives in one flea spare, Where we almost, nay more than married are. *Source:* From "The Flea" by John Donne
Unusual Rhyme (Lesson 35)	A rhyme pattern that does not follow a fixed form, but moves by a pattern determined by the poem. For example, "Fire and Ice" by Robert Frost employs the non-standard rhyme pattern abaabcbdb.
Shortened Sonnet (Lesson 37)	An adapted form of a sonnet, shortened and in the case of "Pied Beauty" by Gerard Manley Hopkins is called a rhymed curtal.
Internal Rhyme (Lesson 41)	Rhyme that appears at the beginning, within, and at the end of lines to create rhythm and unity. THRILLED me—FILLED me with fantastic terrors never felt before; so that now, to STILL the beating of my heart … *Source:* From "The Raven" by Edgar Allan Poe
Alternating Rhyme (Lessons 40, 42)	A pattern where every other line rhymes (either hard or slant rhymes). Bent double, like old beggars under SACKS, Knock-kneed, coughing like hags, we cursed through SLUDGE, Till on the haunting flares we turned our BACKS, And towards our distant rest began to TRUDGE. *Source:* From "Dulce et Decorum Est" by Wilfred Owen

Appendix 5

Positive Points for Potential Poets
by Patricia S. Gray

How do you talk to writers about their own writing? How do you address the "first draft = final copy" syndrome, which many writers—*not just student writers*—seem to develop about the writing of poetry?

Or the "It's my poem, and that's the way I want it" attitude?

Or "It's a poem, and it doesn't need to make sense. I know what it means!" (Lots of kids like to say that!)

We don't want to *discourage* writers from producing potential poems, but then, neither can we honestly tell all writers that their writing is "Super!" "Great!" "Terrific!" ... and other superlatives, if, in fact, the writing still has a way to go. Here are some strategies that *might* help you help budding poets push their poetic writing on toward finished pieces. We should help them perceive their potential poems as works in progress, and we must help them learn that *all* kinds of writing develop through a variety of processes.

Following are some answers to frequently asked questions that you can share with your students.

Can any kind of prewriting become a poem?

I think so.

Can a poem be *about* any subject?

Yes.

Do you have to be "gifted" to write poetry?

NO!

Can I use ordinary words to write poetry?

Yes, but poets try to use ordinary words in extraordinary ways.

How do you know what to write about?

Browse through your brain first, and then through your writer's notebook to find an idea, a thought, or a word, phrase, clause, or even a paragraph, that you might like to *re-create* in poetic form. You don't have to set out to write a poem on purpose; a poem can evolve from other pieces of writing, and poems can take shape from any other kinds of writing. It's the idea, then the words, and then the shaping—all those things make a piece of writing.

Do poems use sentence structure?

Poems have grammar too. Poems can have subjects and verbs. Poets can write complete thoughts. Poets utilize all eight parts of speech! Poems contain syntax, coherence, and unity! Poems use gerunds, infinitives, prepositional phrases, and other sentence elements, just like all effective pieces of writing. Most poets punctuate most poems.

What kinds of subjects are best for poems?

Write about your own personal experiences, which no one else could possibly write about. Use your own idiolect—that is, the language of your life, which is unique to you. Think, *Nobody else in the world has ever put these particular words in this particular order to express this particular thought to achieve this particular effect.* Now that's a powerful thought.

How do you know when a poem sounds just right?

When you write a poem for the first time: Read it aloud, then try to take half the words out.

Read it aloud again. Try to eliminate articles (a, an, the). Conjunctions (fanboys) can usually be dropped.

Read it aloud. Get rid of those wimpy "be" verbs!

Read it aloud. List the first word of each line—what does this list look like? Listen for sounds you like.

Read it aloud. Poems should contain as few words as needed to make the strongest possible statements about their subjects; poets carefully choose each word in a poem.

Ask another person to read your poem aloud to you so that you can listen and hear your own words in someone else's voice. This is vital for you to gain another perspective on what you have written.

> Purposely, and for good reason, **read your poem aloud again and again and again**! Then read it once more—preferably to another human being. Ask a listener, "What did you hear? How did it sound? What struck you? What stayed in your ear?" Avoid asking, "Did you like it?"

Remember—poems are written to be *read aloud*. It's the sound that counts, as well as the meaning, so you want to be absolutely certain that the words you hear are the words you mean!

> True ease in writing comes from art, not chance,
> As those move easiest who have learned to dance.
> 'Tis not enough no harshness gives offense,
> The sound must seem an echo to the sense

Source: From "An Essay on Criticism" by Alexander Pope

Appendix 6

How Can I Improve My Poem?
(Plus Bonus Notes From Laura)

(Let me count the ways …)

1. Color-code your nouns and verbs.
2. Sharpen your nouns and verbs (use a thesaurus).
3. Find your most ordinary nouns and use metaphors for them.
4. Highlight all the visual images and then add one.
5. Try repeating one of your best lines.
6. Add a framed image.
7. Get rid of vague words like *everyone, always,* and *all.*
8. Try playing with white space.
9. Take out some bad rhymes.
10. Take out some good rhymes.
11. Circle all your "to be" verbs and get rid of them.
12. Add a little dialogue.
13. Try switching the order of stanzas or details.
14. Read it to someone and see what confused them.
15. Look for any words you repeat. Get rid of them or change them.
16. Read parts to someone and see if they can finish any of your phrases. If they can, then those are predictable parts. Get rid of them or change them.
17. Trim your adverbs.
18. Trim your adjectives.
19. If you used any color words, make sure they're not the main eight.
20. End with an image that expresses an idea (instead of saying the idea).
21. If your poem mentions words or phrases about tears (especially rolling down cheeks), butterflies in your stomach, or hearts, get rid of them.
22. No kidding. No tears, hearts, butterflies.
23. Listen to your poem. Aloud.
24. Imagine you're a reader, and chunk it up.
25. Get rid of any changes you don't like.

Also ... bonus notes from Laura Van Prooyen:

- You've heard it before, but you'll hear it again. Have students read the work aloud so they can see how it sounds and see where they stumble. I actually compose my own poems by speaking them while I write. It's amazing how you can hear where language is alive and where it falls flat when you read aloud.

  This is especially true for young writers—if you can help them see that there is much more to craft than hard end rhymes, they will grow as readers and writers. Over and over we see that student writers sacrifice image, diction, and metaphor, thinking that they need to rhyme. I'd even go so far as to forbid rhyme for a while to help students train their eye and ear to other ways of crafting a poem.

- Specificity! One of the very best lessons for teaching how to write specific details is Lesson 5, which uses Joe Brainard's "I Remember" as the mentor text. When students are asked to list weird memories specific to them, they really get right to it and engage the senses. I would urge students to look at their drafts (you can tell them that sometimes I work on a poem for *years*! I've never ever published a first draft) and see where they can be more specific, using concrete details that engage the senses. I also love to do exercises with the senses as warm-ups to get students in tune. The best poems are those that we remember long after reading them. I still remember one such poem written by a fifth-grade student who lived near the Nabisco cookie factory in Chicago and described the air as smelling like "brownie pollution." That has stuck with me for years.

Appendix 7

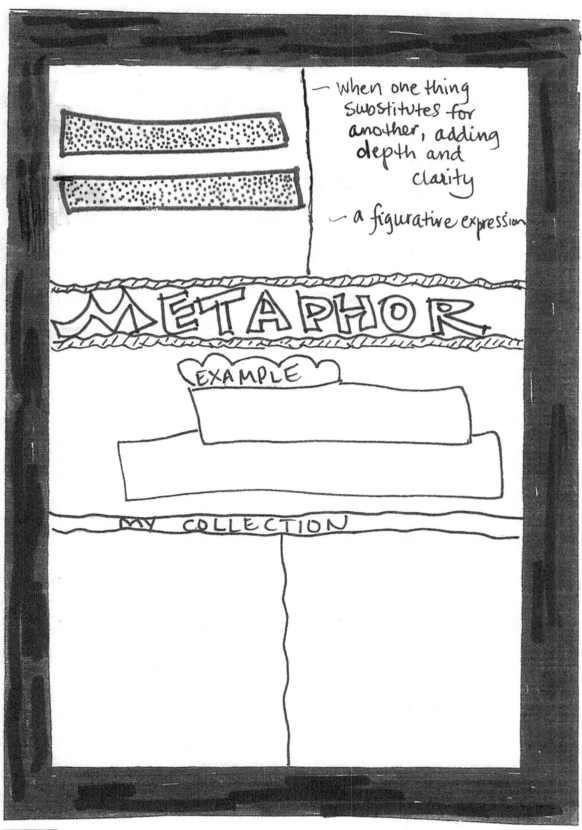

when one thing
substitutes for
another, adding
depth and
clarity

a figurative expression

METAPHOR

EXAMPLE

MY COLLECTION

Appendix 8

Appendix 9

giving non-living things human qualities (like speech)

PERSONIFICATION

EXAMPLE

Plain

Revised

MY COLLECTION

Available for download at **resources.corwin.com/textstructures-poetry**

Appendix 10

Appendix 11

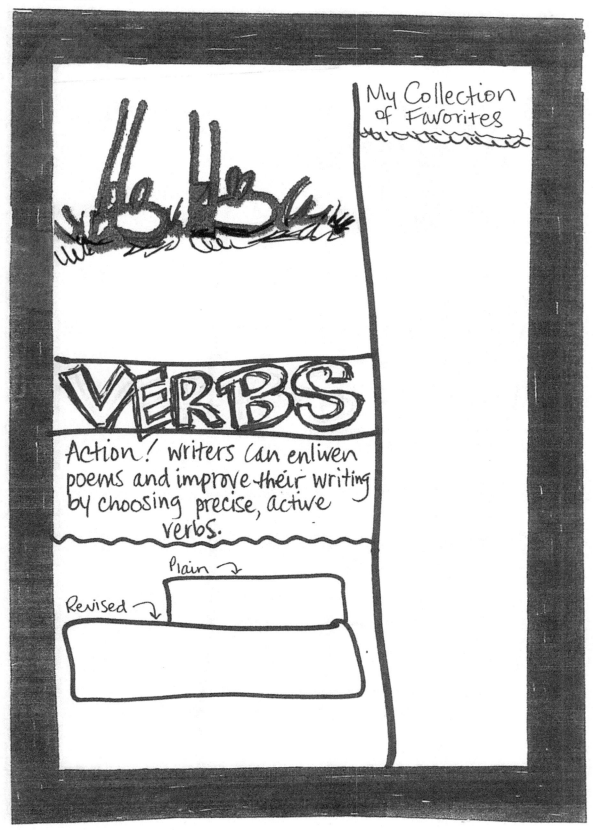

My Collection of Favorites

VERBS

Action! Writers can enliven poems and improve their writing by choosing precise, active verbs.

Plain

Revised

Appendix 12

My Collection of Favorites

VISUAL IMAGE

- A detail that appeals to the senses
- Makes a picture in the reader's mind

Plain →

Revised →

Appendix 13

Reading Lenses and STAAR Stem Questions

> **A Note From Gretchen:** I knew how to help my students with the writing questions on a test, but I didn't know any useful strategies for the reading questions. Enter this strategy. All kids could do it, and we saw so many students who had never passed the reading test before with big old smiles on their faces when they saw they had passed. This strategy is magic. Here is the gist of what you do:

Materials Needed:

Grade-level TEKS

Rigorous grade-level reading selection

Released STAAR questions

Determine the TEKS/objectives that you want to teach. Locate selections that are layered with the skills that you plan to teach.

WHAT HAPPENS IN CLASS

Step One: Read the selection aloud, instructing the students to highlight any terms or vocabulary that they think could be a challenge for anyone in their grade level. Students should also need to pay attention to multi-meaning words as well as words with Greek or Latin roots. After the first read using the vocabulary lens, students will share words that they highlighted, and other students can add those to their lists. This is a great time to discuss context clues, multi-meanings, and Greek/Latin roots.

Step Two: Students read the text again silently. This time a new lens, such as characterization, is added. It is more effective to use a different color to note that this is a different purpose/lens. Again, students are encouraged to make notes about their highlighted characterization text. At this point, another lens could be assigned, such as sensory language, and the process is repeated. *It is up to the teacher and the depth of the selection as to how many lenses can be assigned—dig as far as you can! Students have now not only analyzed a selection but have also found answers for their questions.

Step Three: Use released STAAR questions or other rigorous question banks related to the skills of focus to build question banks for the students. You will need to model how to create a test question by using a stem from an actual test. Allow students to work in pairs or small group initially in order to generate questions. It also helps to provide graphic organizers to aid in the student development of questions.

Step Four: Finesse questions by allowing students to create distractor answer choices in addition to their correct answers. Share questions by allowing students to submit their favorite questions for an assessment, have gallery walks with questions on posters, create notecards with questions that can be organized by skill, and use questions in various centers.

Source: Created by Jennifer Martin. Copyright 2020.

Appendix 14

Meet the Contemporary Authors: Author Fun Facts

LESSON 1: KELLI RUSSELL AGODON, AUTHOR OF "LOVE WALTZ WITH FIREWORKS"

"Love Waltz With Fireworks" was inspired by a memory of seeing a man with argyle socks while eating one of the best cinnamon rolls of my life. I was sitting in a bakery and feeling so grateful for the world around me.

LESSON 2: SARAH ANDERSON, AUTHOR OF "AT THE LAKE"

Sometimes I wake up in the morning with a line running through my head—sometimes it makes sense, and sometimes it doesn't. I try to write it down quickly before I forget it, even if it's nonsense or just one image I remember from my dream. You never know what you might do with that line later.

Regarding writing "At the Lake:" My grandmother told me that if I stuck my thumbnails into the twig of a birch tree and smell the twig, it would smell just like birch beer, a drink I would order at a nearby hamburger spot. And it did. At the time, this was an exciting revelation for me because I loved birch beer. I have a vivid memory of being on my grandmother's dock on the lake where she lived, and her handing me the twig to smell for the first time. So first that twig would remind me of birch beer, and now the smell and taste of birch beer will always remind me of my grandmother. She has been gone for ten years but she remains very much alive in my mind. One thing I love about poetry is that it is a way for me to capture memories and keep experiencing them.

LESSON 3: JIMMY SANTIAGO BACA, AUTHOR OF "I AM OFFERING THIS POEM"

About the poet: Jimmy is an award-winning author who also runs Cedar Tree, Inc., a non-profit educational welcome center where they teach literacy and give books away and run a bookmobile. His latest book of poetry is *Singing at the Gates* (Grove Atlantic, 2019). His poem "I Am Offering This Poem" has been included in the online anthology for the Poetry Out Loud national recitation competition held for high school students nationwide every year (www.poetryoutloud.org).

LESSON 4: SHEILA BLACK, AUTHOR OF "POSSUMS"

One day I heard my dogs barking, and I went outside and found a big dead possum (we have a lot of possums in Texas) lying on its back, with its paws lifted in the air, on my back deck. He was a funny color, too—grayish-white all over, like a ghost. I was pretty scared. This possum was *big*. And what should you even do with a dead possum? Bury him? Throw him in the garbage? I pushed my dogs back and bravely inched forward, but I did carry a long stick. Suddenly, the possum opened one eye. He stared at me a split second, and then—lickety-split—rolled over and waddled away, very fast. (In fact, he hid under my car.) I was so amazed by how well that possum pretended to be dead that I couldn't get it out of my head, so I wrote this poem, "Possums."

LESSON 5: JOE BRAINARD, AUTHOR OF "I REMEMBER"

About the poet: Joe not only wrote but also created paintings, collages, and drawings and designed theatrical sets, costumes, and album covers. He is known most of all for his poetic memoir that begins every single line in the book with the phrase "I remember." People were so inspired by his work that poets and filmmakers created their own art inspired by "I Remember."

LESSON 6: JOANNE DIAZ, AUTHOR OF "MY MOTHER'S TORTILLA"

Secret about writing: I really like rules in poetry, especially when the page is blank and I don't have any fresh ideas. The "rule" for "My Mother's Tortilla" is that I had to create a set of directions for a task and then connect that task to some insight about my mother. Writing about the Spanish tortilla was easy—I had seen my mother make this egg-and-potato goodness for years—but connecting it to her osteoporosis and her imminent demise was trickier. If you're struggling to write a poem, write a "how-to" and see where it goes. The best kinds of how-to poems are the ones that only you can write.

LESSON 7: VIEVEE FRANCIS, AUTHOR OF "STILL LIFE WITH SUMMER SAUSAGE, A BLADE, AND NO BLOOD"

About the poet: Vievee is an award-winning poet originally from Texas who spent many years in Detroit and is now a professor at Dartmouth College. Her work is rich with image and is both fierce and lively, much like the poet herself.

LESSON 8: ANN HUDSON, AUTHOR OF "CHORUS, VENABLE ELEMENTARY"

As a child, I studied my teachers closely. My parents were both teachers, so I had an inkling that my teachers might be regular people after all, but I still couldn't quite imagine it. I watched my teachers and waited for something interesting to happen, and it always did eventually: someone found a wriggly green caterpillar at recess, or we noticed the *tick tock* of my teacher's shoes the day she wore two different black heels to school, or Mrs. King started to cry in music class. I still have the feeling that something interesting is always bound to happen, but you have to watch carefully.

LESSON 9: AUGUST KLEINZAHLER, AUTHOR OF "SNOW IN NORTH JERSEY"

About the poet: August is an award-winning poet known for using conversational and sometimes rough language, who has long reveled in being an outsider. His poems are rich in people and places, offering windows into the worlds he has known, such as in "Snow in North Jersey," where we get to know Mr. Ruiz, Joe, and Myra's boy Tommy, and we come away with a real flavor of the neighborhood.

LESSON 10: AMY LUDWIG VANDERWATER, AUTHOR OF "DRAW"

Every April for the last ten years, as part of National Poetry Month, I have written and shared a daily poem at my blog The Poem Farm. These projects have themes, and in April 2012, I took a "dictionary hike." It worked like this: each day of April, I opened my dictionary to a new letter, beginning with the letter A, and closed my eyes, pointed to a word, and wrote a poem with that word as the title. On April 4, 2012, I pointed to the word *draw*. I looked at the blank page, did not know what to write, and then imagined someone not knowing what to draw. A random dictionary word and a blank page led me to this poem; such writing surprises make me happiest of all!

LESSON 11: NATHAN MCCLAIN, AUTHOR OF "NIGHTHAWKS BY EDWARD HOPPER"

I've attended New York Comic Con for many consecutive years now (I love graphic tee shirts), and one of the tee shirts I bought several years ago was a version of *Nighthawks*, though all the characters on the shirt are from the *Bob's Burgers* cartoon. (People still watch *Bob's Burgers*, right?!)

LESSON 12: ROSE MCLARNEY, AUTHOR OF "FULL CAPACITY"

For a number of years now, I have been imposing forms upon my poems. These are not usually traditional forms, but some constraint on the line count and stanza shape I create for myself, and of which only I may ever be aware. While this sort of structure usually pushes more rigorous examination of my language, in the case of "Full Capacity," because the subject was being confined and I was already making my thoughts conform to the assignment of putting a positive spin on it, I had to break out any consistent form and let the poem sprawl unevenly over the aisles. You've got to know when to change your style (even if what you need to force yourself to do is be freer).

LESSON 13: NAOMI SHIHAB NYE, AUTHOR OF "BECAUSE OF LIBRARIES WE CAN SAY SUCH THINGS"

Regular practice helps. Getting in the habit of writing a few lines in your notebooks every day helps a lot. These lines don't have to be great or even good. They might be the smallest observations. I really like picking up trash to calm my mind every Sunday—it gets me out into the neighborhood, noticing all sorts of things, talking to neighbors I haven't talked to in a long time, cleaning up the place ... this has led to my forthcoming book called *Cast Away, Poems for Our Time*. Find a calming activity you like and stick to it for a while. This helps your writing too.

LESSON 14: MATTHEW OLZMANN, AUTHOR OF "LETTER TO A COCKROACH, NOW DEAD AND MIXED INTO A BAR OF CHOCOLATE"

I don't have any special formula for writing poems, but I try to remind myself that a poem can come from anywhere. The thing that opens the door for a poem to enter the world might be anything. For example, "Letter to a Cockroach, Now Dead and Mixed Into a Bar of Chocolate," owes a debt to the television show *Bones*. I was watching that show and one of the characters mentioned something like, "The average chocolate bar has eight insect legs in it." This wasn't a big part of the show, or even related to the main storyline. But that random fact stuck with me for a while. Much later, I looked it up and found the FDA allows for 60 "insect fragments" in 100 grams of chocolate. Of course, I found that unsettling. I also found it unsettling that we can't see those insect fragments. Eventually, I started to see this as a metaphor. What else can't we see? What other harmful things might we be overlooking or unwilling to see?

LESSON 15: OCTAVIO QUINTANILLA, AUTHOR OF "PARTING"

I wrote "Parting" after reflecting about what it meant for me as a boy to arrive in the United States without my parents. What secret would you like to tell students about your poem? This poem has told me that it loves to be read, and as you now read it, it no longer belongs to me, but to you.

LESSON 16: LESLIE CONTRERAS SCHWARTZ, AUTHOR OF "THE FALCON"

My 9-year-old daughter and I like to write poems together. She's a very funny writer, and so my very serious attempts to talk about the sunset or a blade of grass can quickly turn into imaginative leaps about finding a narwhal as a pen pal or putting bras on camels. (I did have to look up narwhals because I didn't believe horned whales actually existed!) My daughter reminds me to keep a sense of humor, to believe in some magic, and to chase some wild ideas like a kid.

LESSON 17: PATRICIA SMITH, AUTHOR OF "FIXING ON THE NEXT STAR"

About the poet: Patricia is in an award-winning poet who has won the National Poetry Slam as individual champion four times. She is working on a biography of Harriet Tubman and a poetry collection combining text and 19th-century African American photos.

LESSON 18: ANGELA NARCISO TORRES, AUTHOR OF "WHAT I LEARNED THIS WEEK"

I almost always start my poems in my journal, writing "in white heat" with a good pen. When the poem begins to emerge, I open my laptop and take it with me to bed, where, propped on pillows, I type out the poem in lines, allowing the form to emerge organically. I feel like the actual crafting of the poem happens when I'm cocooned in my bed, where I feel most safe and comfortable. Eventually, I will move to my writing desk and "edit in cold blood"—this is where the poem goes through several iterations before I feel it is ready. The adage I quote from above—"write in white heat; edit in cold blood"—is from my college freshman English teacher, who inspired me to be a writer.

LESSON 19: NATALIA TREVIÑO, AUTHOR OF "MARIA"

I miss my hands! Although I can see and feel them all day every day, I cannot always use them for what I want them to do—writing. I could be in the middle of the grocery store picking up lemons, and suddenly, my head and heart will feel a poem coming or a story, or I will fix a problem in my essay, and my hands are nowhere near a notebook! So what happens is it feels like my hands are disconnected from my head! As an English professor by day, a mom, a friend, a daughter, and wife, I am constantly using my hands for so many things, for so many people! And while I love my job and my family, I sure miss my hands. I am sure a lot of working artists miss their hands or their cameras or their paintbrushes all the time, just like me. When my hands are all mine finally, maybe at the end of the day, or very early in the day, and I sit down and write, I feel whole. Because my hands were busy driving out of town the other day to a poetry festival, I wrote a poem in my head. When I got there, I had thirty minutes before my presentation, so I wrote the poem down as I remembered it, and while it took some new turns, it ended where I wanted it to end. It is called "Dear Blue Ford Truck," and of course, it was written to the blue truck who was cruising in front of me, and let me tell you, I had a lot to say to that truck about what we were both seeing and what I imagined we both had seen all our lives. Now, to get my hands back on that poem and revise it—that is what my hands want to do right this minute!

LESSON 20: LAURA VAN PROOYEN, AUTHOR OF "ON THE SHORELINE"

I wrote "On the Shoreline" when I was at a family reunion in Lake Geneva, Wisconsin. I would get up around 5 a.m. to take a walk and clear my head, and then sit and journal (it is bright and sunny so early up north!). One morning it was foggy, and I couldn't tell exactly what I was seeing on the dock. I could see the fishermen on the boat on the lake, or rather I could hear their trolling motor, and I knew what they were doing. But on the dock, I couldn't tell ... but then there it was: a great blue heron. It felt like seeing it was a gift just for me.

LESSON 21: LAURA VAN PROOYEN, AUTHOR OF "AS ALWAYS, THIRTY YEARS BETWEEN US"

I'm not sure why I think it is astonishing that my dad will always and forever be 30 years older than I am, but I do. I mean, it's like we are fixed on a timeline, 30 years apart. Everything that happens in our lives, all of the moments we've experienced and grown, they move along on the timeline with 30 years in between. I never expected to be asked to cut my dad's hair, but he asked me to. And while I did it, I thought of all of the things we've been through.

LESSON 22: LAURA VAN PROOYEN, AUTHOR OF "POSTCARD FROM TEXAS"

About four times a year I will do something called The Grind, where I write a poem a day for a whole month straight. I remember taking a walk in my new hometown, San Antonio, during one of those months when everything was just starting to bloom, but thinking about how back in Chicago, where my parents live, everything was still snowy and cold. It made me really miss them, but also made me grateful I lived where everything smelled nice and was flowering. I wanted to write something to capture that, and if I hadn't been writing a poem a day, I'm not sure I would have sat down to do it. I'm glad I did. That poem was "Postcard From Texas."

LESSON 23: LAURA VAN PROOYEN, AUTHOR OF "ONE OF THOSE DAYS"

The poem "One of Those Days" owes its structure, flow of ideas, and very existence to Barbara Ras and her poem "You Can't Have It All" from the award-winning book *Bite Every Sorrow*. I remain grateful for her model and influence and for creating what became my mentor text. Writers are readers first.

LESSON 24: LAURA VAN PROOYEN, AUTHOR OF "SHE INHERITS HIS STEADY HAND"

It's never a comfortable thing to be with someone who is seriously ill or dying, but I think it is really important to be present and not to shy away and to embrace the multi-generational spaces and places. When the young child in "She Inherits His Steady Hand" is feeding her ill grandfather, she does it with great compassion and empathy, a trait she has inherited from him. It is a real gift to be with and learn from people of all ages, no matter what age you are.

Because...
ALL TEACHERS ARE LEADERS

**GRETCHEN BERNABEI
AND JUDI REIMER**

Building on classic fairy tales, 35 lessons include a writing prompt and a planning framework that leads students to organize writing through a text structure.

**GRETCHEN BERNABEI,
KAYLA SHOOK, AND JAYNE HOVER**

In 53 lessons centered around classic nursery rhymes, this groundbreaking book offers a straightforward framework for guiding young children in their earliest writing efforts.

**GRETCHEN BERNABEI AND
JENNIFER KOPPE**

With 50 short texts written by famous individuals driven by "an itch" to say something, this book provides students with mentor texts to express their own thoughts.

GRETCHEN BERNABEI

This kid-friendly cache of 101 lessons and practice pages helps your students internalize the conventions of correctness once and for all.

To order your copies, visit corwin.com/literacy

Impact your students' literacy skills tomorrow

BERIT GORDON

Discover how to transform your classroom into a vibrant reading environment. This groundbreaking book combines the benefits of classic literature with the motivational power of choice reading.

GRETCHEN BERNABEI AND JUDI REIMER

If ever there were a book to increase students' test scores, this is it. Its 101 student essays and one-page lessons deliver powerhouse instruction on writing well in any genre.

M. COLLEEN CRUZ

By flipping the traditional "reading first, writing second" sequence, these innovative books let you make the most of the writing-to-reading connection with more than 50 carefully matched lesson pairs in each book.

NANCY AKHAVAN

With 75 tasks on beautiful full-color pages, this book offers a literacy instruction plan that ensures students benefit from independent effort and engagement.

A SAGE Publishing Company